THE ENCYCLOPEDIA

OF CALLIGRAPHY

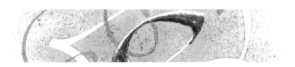

AND ILLUMINATION

THE ENCYCLOPEDIA

OF CALLIGRAPHY

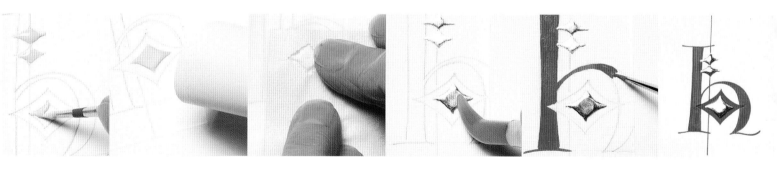

AND ILLUMINATION

A STEP-BY-STEP DIRECTORY OF ALPHABETS, ILLUMINATED LETTERS AND DECORATIVE TECHNIQUES

JANET MEHIGAN & MARY NOBLE

SEARCH PRESS

A QUARTO BOOK

Published in 2005 by Search Press Ltd
Wellwood
North Farm Road
Tunbridge Wells
Kent TN2 3DR

Copyright © 2005 Quarto publishing plc

Reprinted 2006, 2010

ISBN 978-1-84448-064-7

A catalogue record for this book is available
from the British Library.

QUAR.CIL

Conceived, designed, and produced by
Quarto Publishing plc
The Old Brewery
6 Blundell Street
London N7 9BH

Project Editor **Paula McMahon**
Designer and art editor **Elizabeth Healey**
Copy Editor **Claire Waite Brown**
Picture researcher **Claudia Tate**
Photographer **Colin Bowling**
Indexer **Joan Dearnley**
Proofreader **Carol Baker**
Assistant Art Director **Penny Cobb**

Art Director **Moira Clinch**
Publisher **Paul Carslake**

Manufactured by Universal Graphics, Singapore
Printed by SNP Leefung Printing International Limited, China

CONTENTS

INTRODUCTION

Calligraphy has been in use for over two thousand years as a practical and artistic form for man to communicate ideas, history, thoughts and feelings. This book has been developed in response to a recent increasing interest in both calligraphy and illumination. In spite of, or perhaps because of, the fast-advancing computer age, legible, exquisite handwriting is appreciated more now than ever.

INSPIRATION

Calligraphy and illumination are natural partners. We only have to see images of lavishly decorated and illuminated medieval manuscripts to appreciate this. Modern-day scribes have a rich and diverse inheritance of scripts and illustrations from which to choose.

Roman inscriptional lettering was for the glorification of the Empire and its emperors, and the use of later calligraphic writing was a way of communicating religious ideals. It was not long before simple decoration was added to the manuscripts. This provided a practical way of organizing text and the visual impact made it more exciting to read.

Over the centuries different forms of symbolic and decorative expression have accompanied calligraphic styles of writing, pages and pages of which are exquisitely illustrated, decorated and gilded. Some are so delightful that we wish to emulate their expertise. However, each age in history holds its own delights, and the twenty-first century will be no exception. So while we can enjoy studying and copying the wonderful styles of past practitioners, we also need to cultivate and evolve the skills apparent today. We do our ancestors a disservice if our studies are limited to copying and imitation. Copying should be a means of discovering the techniques, and fine-tuning our powers of observation, in order to create something fresh. Today's calligraphers may focus less on the functional aspects of their work and more on the creative side, developing the ancient craft skills and pushing them in new directions.

LEADING BY EXAMPLE

A lot can be learned by trial and error, but the task is always made easier by example and through using a well-produced manual. This book illustrates, by use of

examples and step-by-step instructions, how artistic results can be achieved by anyone who is interested. It is then up to the individual to explore ideas and information, to gradually develop their own creative responses, and progress in their own inimitable way.

The large Gallery houses a superb collection of modern calligraphy and illumination, and illustrates just how diverse the creative spirit is. This work has been produced by some of the most prestigious artists in the field of calligraphic art. As authors we are indebted to the full international spectrum that these artists offer, whether classical, modern, practical or interpretive in execution, and would like to thank them for their generosity in allowing us to utilize their expertise. As an almost endless source of ideas and design combinations, we hope that this very visual section of calligraphic and illuminated excellence will encourage your own journey.

While we have crammed in as much information as possible in the available space, we cannot describe this book as exhaustive. Yet we hope that it will serve a purpose in bringing together both creative inspiration and practical help, all in one volume.

PART ONE

TOOLS AND MATERIALS

ON THE NEXT FEW PAGES YOU WILL SEE SOME OF THE EQUIPMENT MOST CALLIGRAPHERS FIND USEFUL. THERE ARE SEPARATE LISTS FOR CALLIGRAPHY AND FOR ILLUMINATION. MANY ITEMS ARE USEFUL EXTRAS, NOT ESSENTIALS, SO CALLIGRAPHY CAN BE A LOW-BUDGET AFFAIR. HOWEVER, ONCE IT BECOMES A MAJOR HABIT, YOU MAY FIND IT HARD TO PASS BY AN ARTISTS' SUPPLIERS, OR LOOK THROUGH THEIR CATALOGUE, WITHOUT BEING TEMPTED BY THE EXTRAS AVAILABLE, PARTICULARLY FOR PAINTING AND ILLUMINATION. BUILD UP SLOWLY, AND BE PREPARED TO EXPERIMENT TO SEE WHAT CAN BE ACHIEVED.

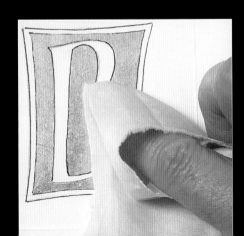

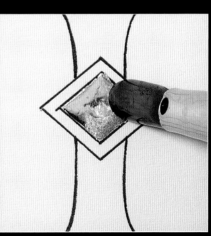

CALLIGRAPHY TOOLS AND MATERIALS

Calligraphy starts easily enough with just a pen, paper and ink. Then there are extra tools and materials that you might want to collect as your interest develops. The most common items can be obtained from stationery stores, but try artists' suppliers for the more specialist equipment.

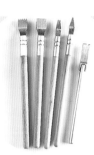

Papers

Layout paper or sheets of photocopier paper are ideal for practising and trying out designs. Cartridge paper is a heavier paper that is suitable for beginners. You will soon want to graduate to watercolour papers with a smooth (hot-pressed) surface, which is ideal both for calligraphy and illumination because the ink or paint sits on the surface, allowing mistakes to be removed. Choose at least 90 lb (190gsm) since thin papers crease easily. "Not" surface (not hot-pressed) is textured and can give pleasing effects. "Rough" watercolour paper is highly textured and harder to write on. Finally, pastel papers are available with various surfaces and in a range of colours. Some will fade, but all are worth exploring.

Dip pens and nibs

The various brands of dip-pen nibs have different properties that are worth investigating. Pen handles are generally interchangeable with the various nibs.

Inks

Always use nonwaterproof, pigment-based bottled inks for permanence. Acrylic inks clog the pen but are ideal for use when diluted for background washes; they dry waterproof giving a "bleedproof" surface on which to write.

Ink stick and ink stone

For the most traditional ink source, use a Japanese or Chinese stick ink, from a reputable source. You will also need an ink stone to reconstitute it. Put a drop of water on the stone and rub the stick in it firmly for two minutes or until sticky. Add more water and repeat as necessary. Dry the stick when finished or it will crack.

Brushes

Pointed and chisel-edged brushes are used for mixing, painting and writing.

Paints

Watercolour paints provide transparent, vibrant colour. Designers' gouache on the other hand is opaque colour that covers well. Bleedproof white paint gives sharper writing than usual white paint.

Water pots

Keep two water pots at hand, one with a dropper for adding clean water to paint, the second for rinsing brushes and pens.

Pencils

HB is the most commonly-used pencil. 2H or harder keeps sharp for ruling lines, while B pencils allow for blacker lines for sketches.

Keep your pencils sharp with a sharpener or craft knife; a compass with attachments is desirable; gum sandarac granules need grinding for treating the paper.

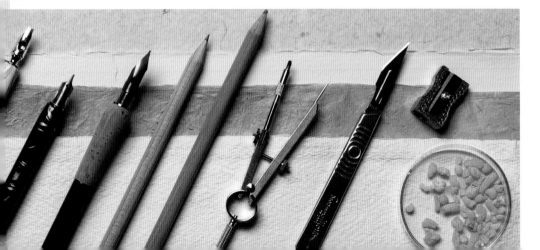

Traditional ink sticks from Japan or China for reconstituting; bottled versions are a convenient alternative. Sticks of colour are also available.

Pencil sharpener
After sharpening with a pencil sharpener, use a knife to finish off the pencil tip if accuracy is important.

Erasers
Soft plastic erasers will remove lines gently. Putty erasers break off and can be used to lift small areas of smudging without disturbing the writing.

Plastic ruler
A plastic ruler with clear markings will enable you to draw accurate lines.

T-square and set square
These tools are invaluable for ruling accurate lines and checking pen angles.

Scissors
To cut paper for paste-ups.

Glue stick
Use "repositionable" glues for paste-ups.

Magic tape and masking tape
Use these to tape ink to the table, paper to the board, and numerous other uses.

Kitchen paper
Kitchen paper has many uses, such as for drying pens after cleaning.

Cutting mat, scalpel and metal ruler
To cut paper sharply and accurately use a scalpel against a metal ruler, working on a cutting mat.

Drawing compass
A drawing compass with a ruling pen attachment allows you to draw circles in ink. Another useful attachment is the metal point which allows pricking regular marks along the edge of paper for ruling lines.

Matches
To prepare a new nib, hold the underside over a flame for four seconds, then drop it into water to stop it overheating.

Old toothbrush
Use a toothbrush to clean nibs. Scrub away from the handle over a water pot, avoiding wetting the handle.

Powdered gum sandarac
This comes as granules which need grinding in a mortar with a pestle to a fine powder (avoid inhaling the dust). Put the powder into a small scrap of finely woven fabric and secure with an elastic band. Pat cloth onto the paper. The fine dust is water-repellent and aids fine lines in writing.

Masking fluid
This rubber solution is used for resist effects. If thinned slightly with water it can be used in a dip pen.

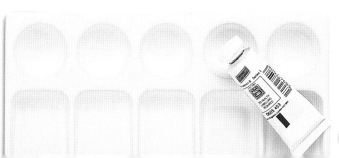

Designers' gouaches are ideal opaque paints for writing; watercolour paints make excellent backgrounds, or they can be used in the pen on white paper.

ILLUMINATION TOOLS AND MATERIALS

Although gouache, artists' and synthetic brushes, and PVA (craft) glue are available from larger stationers, most of the gilding materials used to illuminate letters need to be purchased from specialist art suppliers. These can be found in your local telephone directory, or materials can be sourced by mail order and on the internet. Some suppliers will sell small amounts of gold leaf, however this is not always cost-effective.

Gold leaf

Gold leaf is available in books of 25 leaves. **Transfer gold leaves** are attached to a backing sheet. The leaves of **loose leaf gold** are loose in the pages of the book.

There are two thicknesses of gold leaf, single or double (extra thick), and both should be at least 23½ carats. When gilding, apply single transfer gold first, followed by double loose leaf gold. Keep books of gold safe between pieces of stiff card when not in use.

Shell gold

Shell gold is real gold powder mixed with gum arabic and contained in a small pan. It was originally kept in a shell, hence the name. It can be used to paint fine filigree designs or flat areas of gold for backgrounds.

Gold powder

Gold powder is real gold finely ground into particles. This powder needs to be mixed with gum arabic to make it adhere to the paper or vellum.

Silver leaf

Both transfer and loose leaf can be purchased in books of 25 leaves. Unless coated, silver tarnishes over time with exposure to the atmosphere, taking on a lovely bluish tinge, but eventually turning black. It is also difficult to apply because it has to be laid in a single layer.

Other metals

Platinum, palladium and aluminum are alternatives to silver leaf. The first two are expensive, and aluminum is duller in finish and difficult to handle.

Metallic powders

Gold- and silver-effect metallic powders

Some of the items required for gilding. Eyedropper for adding distilled water to the gesso cake for reconstitution. Dip pen or brushes to apply the gesso to the design. Dog-tooth burnisher for burnishing or polishing the gold to a shine.

NOTE
In the U.S. the attached sheets of gold are known as patent gold, while the unattached sheets are called transfer leaf.

The cheapest and easiest way to gild is to paint using gold or silver gouache, ink or metallic powder that has been mixed with water and gum. Pictured here are gold gouache, silver ink and Trocol metallic powder.

are cheaper than powdered gold. To paint with them you need to add liquid gum arabic and water in order to make them stick to the paper.

Gold and silver gouache

These paints consist of gold or silver metallic powder mixed with gum and contained in tubes. They are easy to use with a brush or a pen, but they have limited shine.

Traditional sizes

Gesso can be used on both skin (vellum) and paper and provides a raised smooth surface on which to apply gold. Slaked plaster of Paris is the essential ingredient of gesso. It can be bought ready-made, or you can make it yourself with dental plaster, water and time (see page 68). Powdered white lead carbonate (this should be handled with great care because it is extremely poisonous), seccotine (fish glue) and sugar are also included in the mix. Distilled water is added for mixing. Armenian bole was traditionally used to colour the gesso, but a little red watercolour paint is a good alternative.

Gum ammoniac can be bought as a ready-made size, or you can make your own with gum ammoniac in lump form and distilled water (see page 70).

Modern sizes

PVA (polyvinyl acetate) glue, also known as craft glue, is a modern size that can be used for raised and flat gilding with gold leaf.

Acrylic and water gold sizes are suitable for flat gilding.

Acrylic gloss medium glue is used for fine gilding.

Gilding tools

A **mortar and pestle** is used to grind the materials for gesso or pigments for paint. Some of the substances are toxic so do not use these tools for anything else.

Measuring spoons are used to accurately measure ingredients for gesso.

Synthetic or nylon brushes, Nos. 1 or 00, should be used to apply gums, ammoniac size or gesso.

A **dip pen** can be used to apply acrylic and water gold sizes, PVA glue and gesso.

A **craft knife** with a rounded blade, or a

Swann Morton scalpel with curved blades Nos. 15 and 15A, should be used for trimming away gesso and unwanted gold.

Scissors for cutting gold leaf must be clean and not used for anything else.

Keep a clean, large **dry brush** for dusting away gold.

Use a **silk square** for polishing gold.

An old **brush** should be used for brushing away pounce or gesso.

Glassine paper (crystal parchment paper) is used to cover gilding while burnishing and to protect your work.

Burnishers

A **medium (24)** and a **small (34) dog-tooth agate burnisher** are the most useful burnishers.

An agate pencil-point burnisher can be used for polishing into tiny crevices and impressing point patterns into the gold (optional).

Haematite or psilomelanite burnishers are the best for burnishing.

An old agate burnisher or stone is used to burnish gesso before applying gold leaf.

Paints and painting tools

Gouache and artists' brushes.

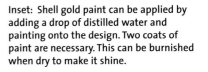

Inset: Shell gold paint can be applied by adding a drop of distilled water and painting onto the design. Two coats of paint are necessary. This can be burnished when dry to make it shine.

GOOD PREPARATION
Before you begin to write, it is a good idea to spend some time preparing your workspace and equipment, so that you can enjoy calligraphy to the fullest: in a comfortable position, with plenty of light, and with working tools.

PREPARING YOUR TOOLS

Try out new dip pens on scrap paper to get a feel for the nib, since different brands will vary. You may find that you need to take a few extra steps to get the nibs ready for flowing calligraphy.

New nibs

If new nibs are coated with a varnish or machine oil that resists the ink, try the "flame treatment". Hold the underside of the nib over the flame of a lighted match for no more than four seconds, then plunge the nib into water (hear it go "pss"). The nib tip should now stay coated with ink when dipped; if not, repeat the process, but don't overheat the metal.

Making marks

Try zigzag patterns to start the nib working. If it seems not to write although filled with ink, a sideways movement will bring the ink from the slit onto the nib edge, where it will then release ink onto the paper. Or simply press, then ease up, before moving the pen along the paper.

To give the ink bottle stability, place it in a hole in a bath sponge.

Burn off varnish and machine oil, but don't overdo it.

Make marks in all directions to get a nib working.

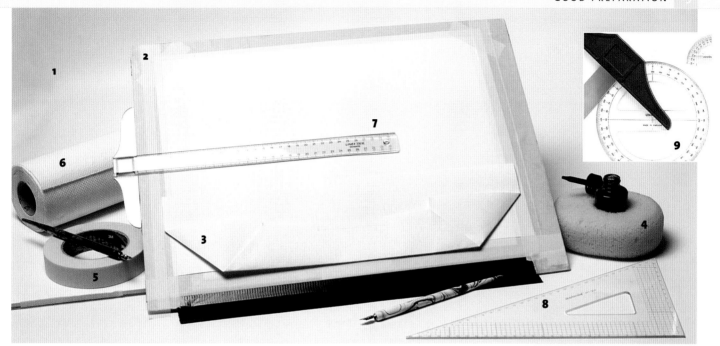

PREPARING A WORKSPACE

You will no doubt be sitting at a desk for long periods of time, so you need to be sure you are comfortable and in the optimal position for producing good work. Here are a few points you need to consider when arranging your working environment.

Desk

It is perfectly possible to write calligraphy on a flat table (1), but a sloped surface (2) is better for posture and for controlling the ink flow from a dip pen. Prop a sheet of plywood – 24 x 18 in. (60 x 45.5cm) or similar – against some books on the table. Pad the writing surface for comfort and smooth writing using eight sheets of ironed newspaper covered with white cartridge or blotting paper. Attach it all to the work surface with masking tape.

Guard sheet

Protect your writing paper from the oils in your hand – which can make the paper slippery – and from drips, using a guard sheet (3). This is simply a strip of paper that covers the part of the surface where your hand rests as you work. Either attach a wide strip across the board using tape, or keep it loose under your hand.

Avoiding and remedying spillage

To avoid spillage, decant a working quantity of ink into a smaller jar or a film canister. Fit this pot into a piece of sponge (4) by cutting a cavity with scissors, or fix it to the table with masking tape (5). Position the ink on the side of your writing hand, so that you don't have to reach over the paper to refill. Keep some kitchen towel (6) or tissues close at hand to clean up any spills of paint or ink, and to dry nibs.

Useful tools

A T-square (7) is valuable for ruling parallel lines, and a set square (8) for checking pen angles. Protractors (9) are also useful for checking pen angles.

Try to write under good light. If you are right-handed, the light needs to come from the left, to avoid casting shadow across your writing. Position the light source from the right if you are left-handed. A small lamp will become a valued accessory.

PART TWO

BASIC PENMANSHIP

GET TO KNOW YOUR TOOLS, AND EXPERIMENT WITH THEM. THE NEXT FEW PAGES COVER THE ESSENTIAL BACKGROUND KNOWLEDGE NEEDED FOR USE WITH ANY OF THE HANDS (SEE PAGES 32–57). USING COLOUR AND BACKGROUND TECHNIQUES ADDS INTEREST TO YOUR WORK, SO IT HELPS TO STUDY HOW COLOURS WORK TOGETHER. PERHAPS THE MOST IMPORTANT AND OFTEN NEGLECTED FACTOR IN A SUCCESSFUL PIECE OF WORK IS DESIGN. KNOWLEDGE OF HOW MUCH SPACE TO LEAVE BETWEEN LINES, WHERE TO PUT YOUR EMPHASIS, AND HOW MUCH MARGIN TO ALLOW, WILL HAVE A MAJOR IMPACT ON THE COMPLETED WORK.

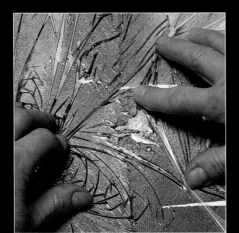

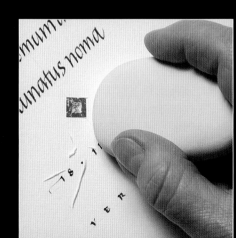

HOW HANDS VARY

This book illustrates ten of the many possible lettering styles that calligraphers can develop. They all derive from historical models and their earliest ancestor is the Roman capital, even though to our modern eye we might think Gothic is older.

An alphabet style is a matching set. There are family characteristics that help the script look well coordinated, and in a lowercase version the key is in the "o" and an arched letter such as "n" or "m". Rhythm in writing is gained by retaining that characteristic throughout the writing.

LETTERING STYLES

Alphabets have developed in varying ways over the ages, and each alphabet has its own recognizable characteristics.

Examine the form

The key to the characteristics of each lowercase alphabet lies in the "o" and an arched letter such as "n". Look carefully at how the "n" is constructed in these examples. What shape is the arch and is it made with a pen-lift or smoothly up from the first stem stroke? Notice how its arch shape (coloured green) mirrors the "o".

Varying weight

Alphabets vary in their weight. In typography terms, that is the difference between a standard type and bold. In calligraphy this is achieved by altering the size of the letters relative to the size of the nib.

Bold and light lower case m's

Note the inside shapes made by italic branching arches, and foundational and Gothic arches, starting from the top, all of which mirror the "O" shape of their family.

How letterforms have changed through the ages (from left to right): Roman, flat uncial, angled-pen uncial, half-uncial, English Carolingian (later revived as foundational), Gothic, French Batarde, italic.

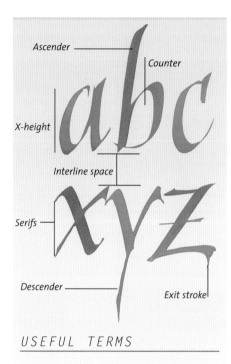

USEFUL TERMS

No matter what letterform you work with, you will surely come across the following terms:

- Counter refers to the shape inside the letter.
- Ascender refers to the part of the letter that extends above the x-height.
- Descender refers to the ascender's counterpart, the part of the letter that extends below the writing line.
- Interline space refers to the gap between x-heights, sometimes governed by the ascender/descender lengths to avoid clashing.
- Serif refers to the little hook at the entry and exit strokes of many letters.
- X-height, also known as body height, refers to the gap between the lines in which the "o" or "x" might fit.

ALLOWING SPACE

Letterforms which have expansive extensions, such as flourished italic, need much more space around them than do blocks of text with no ascenders and descenders. This has design implications, as shown.

Abcdefghyklmnopqrstuvwxyz
zyxwvutsrqponmlkjihgfedcba

Formal italic has long extensions and needs more generous interline space.

Roman capitals can be packed closely together (no ascenders/descenders) but flourished italic needs breathing space.

Gothic needs close spacing, freeform needs lots of room.

Brush capitals work well with minimal interline space.

Uncial's modest ascenders and descenders allow fairly close interline spacing.

RULING LINES
In order to achieve successful and consistent results you need to rule accurate lines. To practise drawing lines, take a sheet of layout paper, a sharp pencil and a good plastic ruler with clear markings. Draw a single horizontal line, this will act as a baseline. Now follow the advice below.

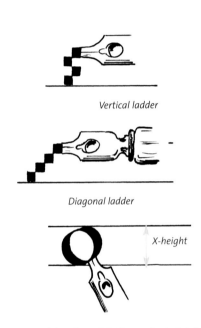

Vertical ladder

Diagonal ladder

X-height

Rule all lines for lowercase letters, but judge capitals and ascenders and descenders by eye

Note the interline space between lines of writing

Capitals and ascenders are not the same height

Rule an extra line if you are using several capitals

How wide should the x-height be?
The distance between the baseline and top line – the lines between which the letters fit without their ascenders or descenders – is known as the x-height and depends on the size of your nib. Each of the alphabets supplied features a scale alongside the "A", indicating how many nib-widths are needed. Hold your pen sideways and make squares in steps or ladders up the page from the baseline. Try this several times if your pen blobs or if you overlap. Once you are sure it is accurate, take this measurement as your figure for ruling up the page.

How much space should there be between lines?
Ruling a whole page of lines that are all the same distance apart is the easiest option. In this instance write on every third line. This leaves a two x-height interline gap, which is usually enough to accommodate ascenders and descenders. When writing mainly lowercase, gauge the height of ascenders and occasional capitals by eye, to avoid ruling extra lines that will confuse your work. You should only add an extra line for capitals if a whole word or more is to be written completely in capitals. Note that ascenders are marginally higher than capitals in many alphabets.

RULING UP THE PAGE

When you are practising on thin paper, you could rule one set of lines (heavily) and keep it underneath, to save time. For finished work on thicker paper, and for very narrow lines, you will need to rule up the actual writing page.

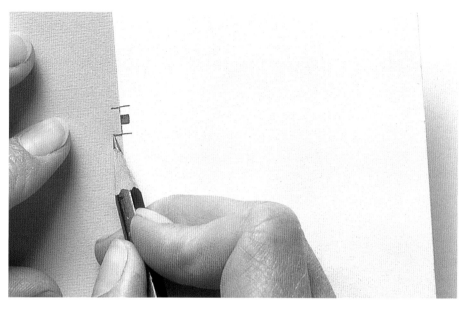

3 Alternatively, use the straight edge of a strip of paper to accurately take the measurement.

1 Take a measurement from your nib-width ladder, using a ruler or dividers.

2 Rule your first line, then mark with a ruler or dividers down the page to repeat the measurement.

4 Align the strip and use in the same way as for dividers. Do this at each end for parallel lines unless using a T square.

5 Establish the interline space – it is simplest if this is a multiple of the x-height. Mark x-heights and interline spaces down the page and rule lines across.

USING COLOUR

Colour in the pen can enliven and enhance your calligraphy, but remember it will not mask poor letterforms! Start simply, with one colour, then develop your colour mixing and blending skills to put harmonious colours together.

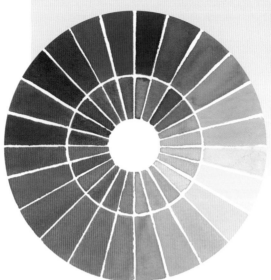

Bottled inks

Bottled inks come ready to use, but are usually transparent and so will not show up against coloured backgrounds. Inks are generally dye-based, and subject to fading so take care not to rely on them for finished work that you may want to put in display.

Watercolours

Watercolours can be used both for writing and painting illuminations. Like coloured inks, they are transparent, so they work best on white paper. The colours are bright and are excellent for mixing. The pigments used are designed to last, so are light-fast (check the label). When using tubes, squeeze out a small quantity and add water by the brushful until it is of ink consistency. If you use pans, wet your

brush and keep rubbing the pan with water until you have enough colour on your brush to load your pen. For painting, transfer some paint to a mixing dish so you can mix it with other colours.

Designers' gouache

Designers' gouache is an opaque colour which will show up well against any background, so it is ideal for calligraphy, and also for illumination, particularly where a flat, even colour is needed. Check the label for its light-fastness rating. To mix the paint to the right consistency, squeeze about 5mm length of paint onto a dish and add water a brushful at a time until it is runny but still thicker than your black ink. Test its writing with the pen. If the pen seems reluctant to write, the paint may need another brushful of water. Keep going until it writes well, but maintains strong colour. If you have to water it down too much it will lose its opacity, which you need for writing on coloured backgrounds.

Pans of watercolours

COLOUR WHEEL

If you are not familiar with using colours, play safe at first and use colours that are close in the colour wheel. For example, the following demonstrations use blue-green gouaches – cobalt blue and viridian mixed and with a touch of lemon. They are all adjacent colours on the wheel. The coloured pencil infills are more daring, exploring contrast, as the yellow moves us further round the wheel, and the orange used as highlight is directly opposite.

FEEDING THE PEN

1 Mix gouache with water to a "single cream" consistency and feed the pen by stroking the brush across the edge of the pen's reservoir. Add more water to the mix if the pen feels different from when you used black ink, but take care not to make the colour too thin.

2 Write slowly and concentrate on good letterforms. Keep recharging the pen with colour well before it starts to run out, to maintain evenness of colour. Aim for an opaque coverage preferably of gouache, not watery, transparent colour.

USING CHALK-BASED PASTELS

1 Chalk-based pastels offer a simple but effective colour effect. Prepare your writing first, and erase all your lines, as erasure after laying pastel will take the pastel off again! Select a suitable colour and scrape the pastel with a craft knife over the area.

2 Gently rub the grated pastel into the paper with a soft tissue or cotton wool, pushing into the paper, not just dusting it off. If the first effect is not strong colour, repeat the process several times. Try two colours, selecting ones that blend well together (check the colour wheel).

USING COLOURED PENCIL

Select two harmonious colours in coloured pencils and carefully fill in the counter spaces with the first pencil, leaving an even white gap all round. Add the second (orange) colour along the top only.

GRADATED LETTERFORMS

For colour change in the writing, you need several mixes of colour of all the same consistency, and chosen to blend well together. Feed the pen with the first colour and after a few strokes recharge the pen with the next colour. Experience will tell you how frequently to change.

BACKGROUND WASHES

Creating visual interest by using colour behind your calligraphy can be an extremely effective means of enhancing a design. Take care to choose colours that go well together and try not to overwork the background. The following are examples of some of the background effects that can be achieved with watercolour paints. You can explore them all, and even try combining them.

1 **Plastic wrap** For a frosty, crinkly texture, lay plastic food wrap on the wet surface and move it around until well creased.

1 **Variegated wash** Using watercolour paint and plenty of water you can brush on a wash of colours that blend together. If you do not wish to stretch paper for washes, use a heavyweight watercolour paper that will not wrinkle.

2 Add more colours in the same way, keeping an eye on how well they blend together.

2 Leave it in place until the paint is dry, then peel the wrap off gently.

1 Sponging Use a coarse sponge to apply watercolour paint for variety of texture, here shown applied over still-wet earlier layers.

2 Alternatively, for sharper marks, allow the first sponging to dry before adding the next layer of watercolour.

1 Wet-in-wet This is a fun and unpredictable technique. Use a well-loaded brush to drop a strong colour onto wet paper, then drop in another colour.

2 To make the colour disperse further, blow onto the paint through a straw. The final effect is impossible to reproduce, and it is fun to see what emerges.

This one is so striking it serves as a picture, so a short quote about a tree, written underneath, might suit.

Masking fluid resist Masking fluid provides a resist to watercolour paints, and can be used in decorative ways. Spatter masking fluid over dry paper, perhaps with an object masking some areas. When it is dry, apply a watercolour wash over it (see left). When the wash is dry, use your finger to gently remove the masking fluid and reveal speckles of white in the wash.

Explore all these techniques, and try combining them – spattered paint over a variegated wash, or sponged colours over the masking fluid.

LAYOUT PRINCIPLES

The placing of words on the page has as much influence on the success of a piece of calligraphy as the skill in its writing. It is important that the whole arrangement is seen as a definable shape, so that it works as a unit. Think about the feel of the piece and jot down some ideas about how the words could be arranged.

Above: centred gives a traditional, balanced arrangement.

Right: Insetting a "dropped capital" is a traditional device. You will need to do some trials with this motif to achieve a balanced arrangement.

Above: ranged right makes it harder to achieve an even right margin.

Above: ranged left works well with even lengths of line.

Margins

It is always tempting to fill up the whole page, but this is only appropriate when aiming for an overall texture. If there is a definable shape to the piece, it must be allowed to show by leaving sufficient space all around it. A rule of thumb could be to measure the widest space between any two lines of writing, double it, and make that your top margin. The sides should be a little wider, and the bottom margin should be the widest, perhaps twice the top margin.

Alignment

We are familiar, thanks to layouts in print, with the choice of left-aligned, right-aligned, and centred text positions. These are devices we use frequently in calligraphy. For a first piece, left-aligned saves too much measuring. The right-aligned option is the hardest to achieve, while for a centred design always use a paste-up.

Sketches

Sketch some first thoughts for an arrangement, using a soft pencil, trying landscape and portrait layouts, before doing any writing.

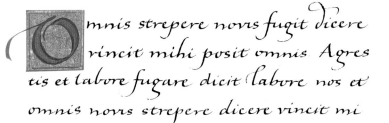

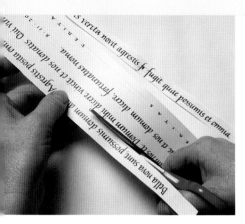

PASTE-UPS

1 Write out all the text and cut it out in strips, cutting any mistakes off as well.

2 To create a centred layout, rule a centre line on a fresh sheet of paper. Lay your text strips roughly on the page, cutting up any lines that are too long, and move them about to find a balance. Fold the strips in half to find their centre, then glue them, lining up the crease with the centre line.

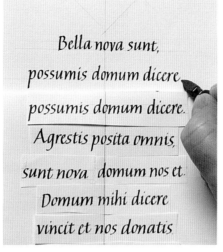

3 Rule lines on the final "best" sheet, including a centre line. Position your paste-up on top, folded to show the first line aligning to the centres. Write in "best", checking where to start and finish. Fold and repeat for all lines.

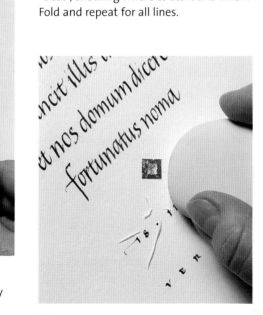

4 When the final piece is complete, let the ink dry before carefully erasing the ruled lines.

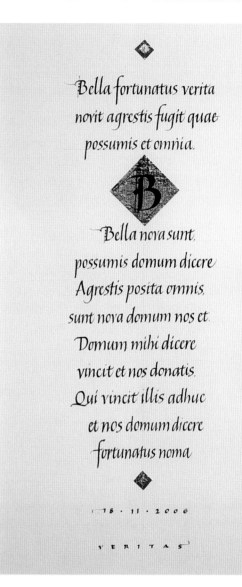

The final version, with decorative diamonds and initial B added last.

SEE ALSO

◉ Ruling lines page 20

TEXTURE TECHNIQUES

Sometimes we want a more dramatic backdrop for our calligraphy, and here are some simple but effective ideas. These are fun techniques that never turn out the same twice, so you will need to respond to the textures you produce with appropriate placing of the calligraphy.

USING CONTRAST

Experienced calligraphers like to explore the greater possibilities that the contrast of weight, size and style of writing can give to a design. Italic and Roman capitals are the best source of lettering for these variations.

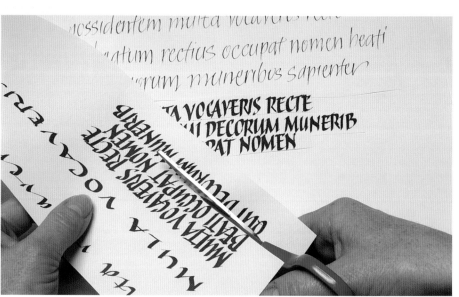

2 Cut out contrasting weights of lettering – irrespective of what they say.

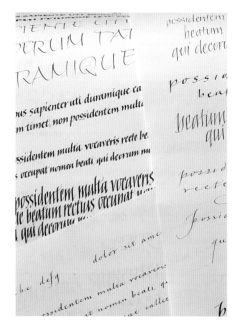

1 Start off with a selection of text – here italic and Roman capitals – encompassing various weights and sizes of letter. This Latin quote becomes random text as paste-ups develop for visual effect.

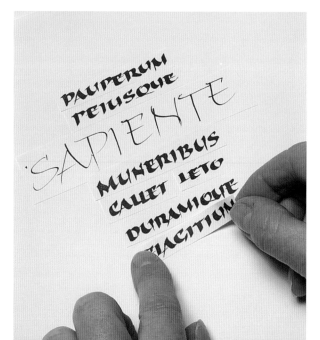

3 Try gaining contrast in a "portrait" layout with heavy- and lightweight lettering setting each other off. This would be less successful if there were equal quantities of each weight.

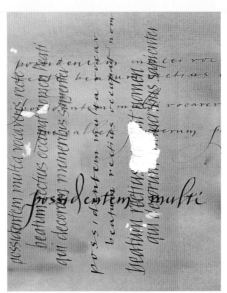

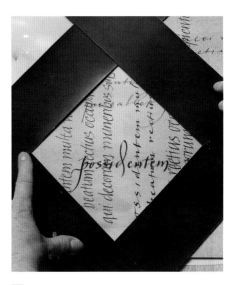

4 Another idea, this time in "landscape", uses lightweight text counterbalanced with heavier title words.

6 The overlaid texts make interesting visual patterning, which can be easily moved, and coloured backgrounds can be explored.

7 Use "L"-shaped corners to decide the final cropping of the design, and don't be afraid to explore unusual options.

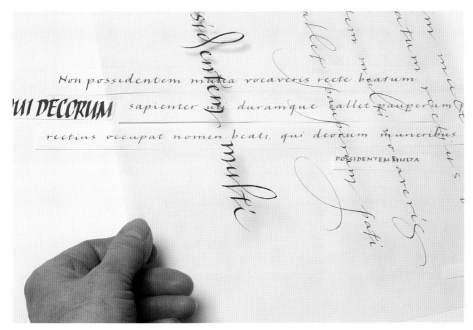

5 Try photocopying the writing onto acetates that can be moved around the page to encourage more ideas.

CREATIVE EXPRESSION

Look in the Gallery for examples such as this one by Nadia Hlibka, which illustrate a freer approach to design. Areas of lettering as texture counterbalance each other and combine with images and colour for creative expression.

PART THREE

THE HANDS

BEGINNERS ARE SOMETIMES SURPRISED TO DISCOVER THAT
CALLIGRAPHY IS USUALLY WRITTEN MUCH MORE SLOWLY THAN
REGULAR HANDWRITING. SLOW, CAREFUL WRITING ALLOWS ATTENTION
TO THE SUBTLETIES OF FORM, WHICH DIFFER IN EACH ALPHABET. EACH
OF THESE HANDS IS SHOWN AS A FULL ALPHABET, WITH REPRESENTATIVE
LETTERS DEMONSTRATED IN STEPS. PAY SPECIAL ATTENTION TO THESE
EXAMPLES, AND TO THE PEN ANGLE SHOWN, AS THIS DIFFERS WITH
EACH HAND. SOME OF THE DIFFERENCES OF FAMILY CHARACTERISTICS
IN THE ALPHABETS ARE QUITE SUBTLE, SO TAKE YOUR TIME AND
CONCENTRATE ON ONE HAND UNTIL YOU ARE FAMILIAR WITH IT,
BEFORE TRYING ANOTHER.

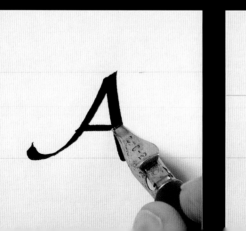

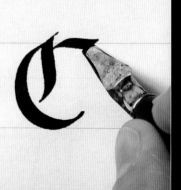

FOUNDATIONAL
Also known as roundhand, this is a classic minuscule hand that every calligrapher uses for projects where legibility is the first priority. Study the text in this book and you will recognize how closely many modern fonts are modelled on this style, which originates in the tenth century.

COMPOSITION

- Shown here at 4 nib-widths, sometimes 4 ½ is appropriate.
- The letters are upright and very rounded, giving a characteristically high-arch formation on "h", "m", "n" and "u".

- The arches are the element that distinguishes foundational from italic, with which it is sometimes confused by beginners, so it is important to be aware of the difference.

- The governing shape for all the letters is "o" – if only in their width – although "g's" bowl is smaller. The "r" is an "n" that's stopped short.

PRACTISING THE LETTERFORMS

Concentrate on "n" and "o" until you can write them consistently with the thin parts on "o" at about 11 and 5 o'clock, and the arches on "n" high up. If your paper is thin enough, lay a fresh sheet on top of your best "o" and form "n" on top of it. You should be able to make most of the alphabet this way – remembering that the "o" of the "g" is smaller – for example, "f" and "j" have "o" in their curves, while "s" fits into the circle, as does "a".

Write the letters at a 30-degree pen angle, apart from "w".

m h, n, r	**b** l, o, t	**w** k, v, x, y	**g** s

1 With a small curved serif, make a straight downstroke.

1 Start with a small serif 3 nib-widths above the top line, then work straight down, but stop short of the baseline.

1 Start with a small serif, then use a steep pen angle for the first stroke.

1 Make a small "o" attached to the top line.

2 Start the arch inside the top of the stem. Make the arch rounded, like the top of "o", then pull down. Finish with a rounded foot.

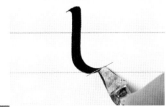

2 Make a curve as you would for the corner of "o".

2 Blend the second stroke into the first at the base.

2 A long curvilinear stroke completes the "o" and starts the tail.

3 Repeat Step 2 for the second stroke.

3 Return to the stem, just below the top line, and complete the "o" shape with a round stroke.

3 Repeat the "v", with the serif on the final stroke.

3 Curve back to close the tail, but don't let it hang too low.

ROMAN CAPITALS
These are the original classical letterforms, introduced by the Romans, hence their name. A classical version would be at 7 or 8 nib-widths. They can accompany any other letterform, in particular at 6 nib-widths with foundational hand. Maintain a constant 30-degree pen angle, except where shown for thicker or thinner strokes. Vary the weight by experimenting with nib-widths.

COMPOSITION

- Shown here at 6 nib-widths, these letters are very geometric in formation, based on the square and the circle.

- With a few exceptions, letters can be divided into several groups:
  round, "O", "Q", "C", "G", "D";
  half the width of the square, "E", "F", "L", "B", "P", "R", "K", "J", "S";

three-quarters of the square, "H", "A", "V", "N", "T", "U", "X", "Y", "Z".
- Of the exceptions: "M" fits the square, "W" bursts out of the square, and "I" is too thin to count.

PRACTISING THE LETTERFORMS

Study the compositional groups listed with their widths in mind. Graph paper may be helpful at the start, but avoid becoming dependent upon it. Instead, make a gauge to check your widths. To do this take a scrap of paper or card, mark on it the nib-width height of the writing lines, then fold it to find the centre and fold again to find the three-quarter mark. Check your widths by holding this gauge across each letter you write.

Write the letters at a 30-degree pen angle, except parts of the "M".

E F, H, I, L, T	**G** C, O, Q	**B** D, P, R	**M** N, V, W

1 Make a straight stem with optional serif. Lift the pen.

1 Start just below the top line with a strong "C" curve.

1 Make an upright as with "E" but bring it round to the right.

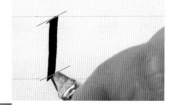

1 Use a steeper pen angle for the first upright, which needs to be slim.

2 Make a horizontal crossbar starting to the left of the upright. At 30 degrees this should look thinner than the upright.

2 Flatten the top curve and end in a small serif.

flatter

2 Make a small upper bowl that finishes before halfway and does not meet the stem.

2 Make a wide "V" with strokes at the usual pen angle.

3 Make another two crossbars, but end them with tiny hook serifs.

3 To draw the stem, move across and down and blend into the "C" shape at the base.

3 Make a larger lower bowl and blend it into the first stroke.

3 Complete the last upright with a minimal outward splay.

UNCIAL

UNCIAL Based on scripts that evolved between the third and ninth centuries, this is a complete hand without separate capitals and lowercase letters. Keep all the letters very rounded and use a flat pen angle. There are two versions of some letters to give the option of a modern or more historic look. Uncials are often associated with Christianity, because they spread with the copying of early Bibles.

COMPOSITION

- Shown here at 4 nib-widths, you could also experiment with a very chunky 3 nib-width version.
- Every letter has the round "o" within it, so do not be tempted to squash them up. The serifs should be minimal.

- Using lighter weights, such as 5 or 6 nib-widths, gives an interesting contrast, but makes it harder to maintain the roundness and flat pen angle.

- The following examples are the more difficult letters in this hand.

PRACTISING THE LETTERFORMS

Practise "o" first, since this is the governing shape. Note where the thin parts occur, at 5 and 11 o'clock, and adjust your pen angle if they occur elsewhere. If you use thin practice paper you can then put a good "o" underneath and write the other letters to conform to the round shape. Remember these are capitals, so the ascenders and descenders should be minimal in their extensions.

Write the letters at a 25-degree pen angle, with some steeper twists on "a" and "w".

o c, e, g	**w** m, t, u	**a** k, v, x, &	**r** b, p

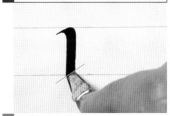

1 Start below the top line with a smooth curve.

1 Make a tiny hook serif then a rounded curve a little flatter than with "o."

1 Make a small serif and a straight diagonal, avoiding waviness, and end with a small serif.

1 Make a small serif and a strong straight stem.

steeper

45°

2 Join inside the first mark, and pull up and round. "c" and "e" are formed in the same way.

2 Repeat for the second curve, ensuring it joins with no gap.

2 Pull out in a curve from inside the first stroke.

2 Start from inside the stem and pull out, slightly branched. "n" and "h" share a similar form.

45°

3 Complete the curve by overlapping seamlessly.

3 Make the last stem stroke with minimal entry and exit serifs.

3 Curve back and twist the nib a little for a smooth join.

3 Finish with the foot, keeping it an open letter to preserve its roundness.

CAROLINGIAN

This is a wide, shallow minuscule hand with tall ascenders, and several letterforms akin to uncial. Roman capitals are an appropriate accompaniment, at 5 or 6 nib-widths. Carolingian is particularly suitable for small writing, since its roundness and simplicity make it very legible at even a few millimetres high. The historical version has heavier serifs on ascenders, as shown here with "l".

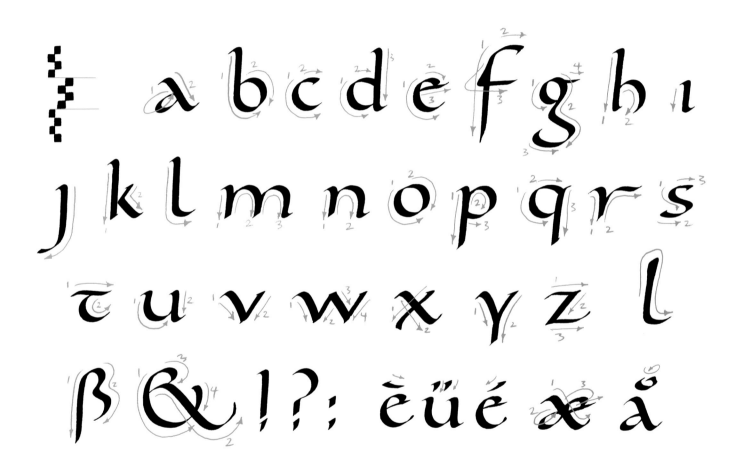

COMPOSITION

■ Here shown at 4 nib-widths high, 3 or 3½ would also be acceptable; adjust the height of the ascenders and accompanying capitals accordingly.

■ The hand is based on a very round "o", almost wider than high, and uses a flat pen angle and high branching arches. The arches are made without pen-lifts, as in italic, but are rounded and high, more akin to foundational. Some of the forms are also like uncial – "a", "e", "h", "t", "y".

PRACTISING THE LETTERFORMS

Accustom yourself to the round "o" and make all the letters as wide as you can bear. Letters "m" and "n" need attention to obtain the high arch that branches from the base but does not emerge until high up. The entry stroke starts with a small serif. However, if you prefer the historical ascender, use an up-and-down movement that demands a light touch with a well-inked pen.

Write the letters mostly at a 30-degree pen angle, except for "w".

d o, p, q	**l** b, d, h, k	**m** h, n, r	**w** k, v, x, y, z

1 Start a very rounded bowl just below the top line.	**1** This is an example of the alternative, historical ascender, which starts with an upward stroke.	**1** Make a small serif and a straight stem stroke then lift the pen off cleanly.	**1** Make a small serif then pull a strong, downward, diagonal stroke.

2 Make a flat top lined up with the first stroke's width.	**2** Bring the pen down so this stroke is strong and straight.	**2** Bring the pen in a branching stroke from the stem, in a wide rounded arch.	**2** Blend the second diagonal into the first stroke and check that your pen angle is still flat.
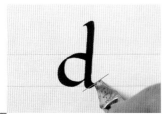			
3 Make the ascender with a small serif, a long straight downstroke, and a final small serif.	**3** For "l" and "b", make an elegant curve before reaching the baseline.	**3** Repeat for the second arch, with a small finishing serif.	**3** Repeat the "v" again, checking width and pen angle, and make seamless joins.

GOTHIC
This page shows a basic minuscule alphabet that should be used with the capitals on pages 42–43. This is a regular, solidly textured hand, which when written as words should look like a picket fence of evenly spaced uprights. Gothic comes into its own for an authentic medieval look and sets off the elaborate capitals. It is not particularly legible, so do not use it for text that requires quick reading.

COMPOSITION

- Think of this as a "modular" letterform. Note how many letters are composed strictly of a short, diagonal, diamond shape, attached to a heavy vertical stem.

This can be seen clearly when comparing "m", "n", "u", "v" and "w" – look at them upside down, only one diamond or a small gap differentiates them.

- Keep the ascenders and descenders as minimal extensions beyond the x-height, because this is a compact hand with single x-height interline space.

PRACTISING THE LETTERFORMS

Copy "i" many times, to get the three modular strokes firmly into a rhythm, before transferring that format to the many other letters that share the shape. Maintain a regular distance between all the upright strokes (stems), so take care not to make the letters too open. The counter (gap inside the letter) should be approximately the same width as the uprights.

Write the letters at a 40-degree pen angle, apart from "s".

| **o** a, c, p, q | **m** b, h, u, v, w | **g** y | **s** z |

1 Start a straight stroke below the top line and stop it before the baseline.

1 Start with a diagonal diamond, then pull a straight and another diamond diagonal as for "o".

1 Just as in "o", start a straight stroke below the top line , then make a short diagonal stroke.

1 Starting below the top line, form half a stem stroke, then a diamond, then a stem to the baseline.

2 Use a short, diagonal, diamond-shaped stroke to take it to the baseline.

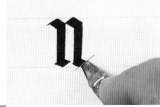

2 Repeat the same three strokes but allow a gap at the bottom, making "n".

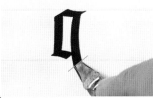

2 Form the bowl as if you are completing an "o", but slightly curving the upright. Continue below the baseline.

2 Elegantly curve the bottom stroke to meet the stem at the baseline, not overlapping.

3 Repeat these shapes, short then long, keeping the gap between the uprights narrow.

3 Repeat again to turn "n" into "m".

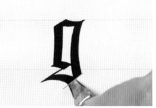

3 Make a thin sideways stroke, then curve diagonally to join at the bottom.

3 Complete the top with a diamond and serif.

GOTHIC CAPITALS

These highly ornamental capitals should be used sparingly, for example as initials, and never for whole words since they may be indecipherable. In a block of minuscule text, a capital provides visual contrast from all the straight lines, like a gate in a picket fence. If these letters fascinate you, there are many other versions to be found in calligraphy books and medieval manuscripts.

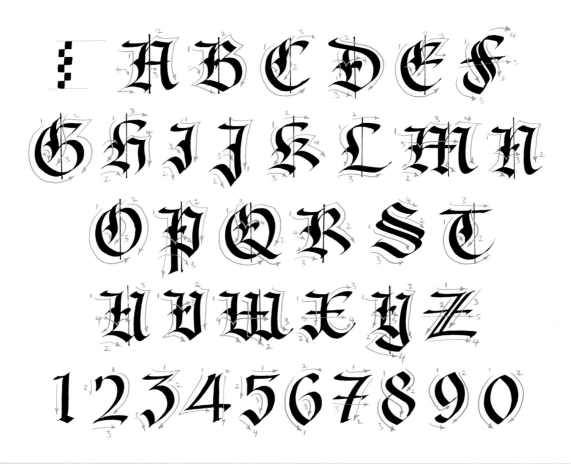

COMPOSITION

- These letters are intentionally much wider and more curvilinear than their minuscule counterparts. Some variation in pen angle is necessary to create these letters, most obviously in the optional thin vertical line, achieved by turning the pen sideways to utilize its thinnest axis.

- Make the letters 1 or 2 nib-widths higher than the lower case.

PRACTISING THE LETTERFORMS

Try the rounded letters first, especially if you have been writing the minuscules for any length of time, since you will need to get used to the much wider, expansive shapes. Study the letters in groups that share similar strokes to build up a concept of logical construction. The thin line is optional, as is the decorative "thorn", or you can add more, to suit your needs.

Write the letters at a 40-degree pen angle.

G C, E, O, Q, T	**H** K, L	**M** N, U, V	**S** F
			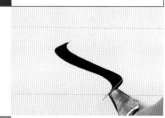
1 Start with a wavy upright, then make a smooth curve from the top line round, as with "C".	**1** Make a wavy stroke from the top line to the baseline, then make the hooked foot.	**1** Make a short horizontal entry stroke, a slightly wavy downstroke, then a "foot".	**1** Starting a nib-width below the top line, make a long diagonal with minimal serifs, ending on the baseline.

2 Add the top "lid" on. See also "C" and "E".	**2** Complete the top stroke like a "C", and add a decorative "thorn".	**2** Turn this into "N" with horizontal, vertical and foot strokes.	**2** Make a parallel stroke below this, ending on the baseline.

3 From the top lid form a sideways hairline, then complete the curve to join to the base. Turn the pen sideways to form the thin vertical line.	**3** Make a horizontal stroke, then move down to just penetrate the baseline.	**3** Repeat to make "M", but curve the exit stroke. Add the decorative horizontal.	**3** Make the base and top strokes with elegant slight curves.

FORMAL ITALIC

This formal minuscule alphabet has rhythmic up-and-down branching strokes. Each letter is formed individually, but with fewer pen-lifts than in many other hands, revealing a close relationship to joined-up handwriting. It is possible to study this hand with a view to improving one's handwriting, with much practice. The joins should be regular and branching, like "n" and "u".

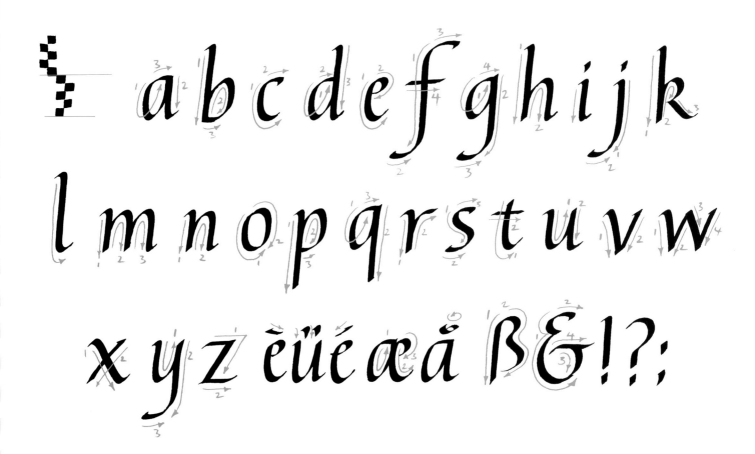

COMPOSITION

- Generally 5 nib-widths in x-height, with ascenders and descenders also up to 5 nib-widths. The letters "a", "n" and "o" hold the most characteristic features.

- The letters are narrow, sloping and branching. Branching involves keeping the pen on the page between the downstroke and branching upstroke, emerging from the stem at halfway. The slope should be consistent, but could be between 5 and 12 degrees from the vertical.

PRACTISING THE LETTERFORMS

Before attempting the letters shown below, get used to making the pen write upwards without digging into the paper or becoming too scratchy. This is essential for the characteristic branching of this hand. Write lots of "u" shapes, well lubricated with ink, and concentrate on lightening the pressure on the pen to allow it to glide upwards. If it remains scratchy, gently blunt the right-hand edge of the nib only on fine sandpaper, until it glides more smoothly.

Write the letters at a 45-degree pen angle.

a d, g, q, y	o c, e	f g, t, y	m b, h, p, r

1 Starting just below the top line, make a sweeping down-and-up stroke all the way to the top.

1 Start below the top line with a sweeping curve, ending in a hairline stroke.

1 Follow this method for all ascenders and descenders. Start on a hairline and maintain a straight stem all the way down.

1 Make a small serif and straight stem, then make a clean stop.

2 Bring the pen down again parallel to the first stroke and lift off upwards.

2 Place the pen in the thicker part of the first stroke to blend a seamless join.

2 Complete the descender with a blending stroke.

2 Bring the pen up from the bottom, emerging halfway and making an asymmetric arch.

3 Blend in the top with an upwards stroke.

3 Complete the right-hand curve, blending into the bottom curve.

3 Add the top stroke, blending it into the stem, then form the crossbar sitting under the top line.

3 Repeat the movement to turn "n" into "m", and finish with a small serif.

FORMAL ITALIC CAPITALS

The italic capitals share the same shapes as Roman capitals but are more compressed in width, and have the same characteristic slope as the formal italic minuscules. They are strong but very simple, and their forward slope gives a slight informality often favoured in modern calligraphic works where all capitals are called for.

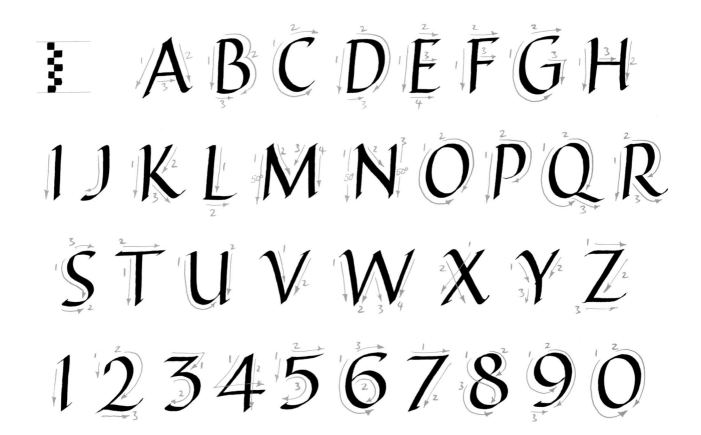

COMPOSITION

- Generally 7 nib-widths, but variable to suit the context. When used in conjunction with the minuscule, ensure that they are in proportion and remain shallower than the height of ascenders.

- Note: The pen angle is 30 degrees, as it is for Roman capitals, and not 45 degrees as it is for italic lowercase.

PRACTISING THE LETTERFORMS

If you are familiar with Roman capitals, then remember that the relative widths of the letters are important. All the "O" shapes, "O", "Q", "C", "G" and "D" should share the same oval curve shape.

Ensure that "E", "F", "L", "J" and "S" are narrow, and that "B", "P" and "R" share a similar width, although the visual midpoint is different for each.

Write the letters at a 30-degree pen angle.

H E, F, I, L, T	**O** C, G, O	**A** V, W, X, Y, Z	**R** B, D, P, K

1 Start with a small serif and make a straight stroke.

1 Start below the top line with a sideways pen movement describing the oval.

1 At 30 degrees the first diagonal is a thin stroke.

1 First make a straight stroke with no serifs.

2 Make a parallel stroke to establish the width.

2 Place the pen inside the thicker part of the first stroke and join to complete the oval.

2 The second diagonal will be thicker. End it with a serif.

2 Start the top bowl slightly to the left of the upright, to gain a strong join.

3 Join with a horizontal cross-stroke. Note the relative thickness.

3 To turn "O" into "Q" add the diagonal stroke but join with a hairline serif.

3 Still at 30 degrees, the horizontal crossbar will be thin.

3 Bring the foot out straight, not bending, and without touching the upright stem.

FLOURISHED ITALIC
This is a much livelier version of the formal italic, and it is necessary to have gained a thorough understanding of the latter before embarking on these more exuberant characters. These are fun to write, but demand more control than may be apparent. For most applications exercise restraint – less is more, do not create spaghetti if you strive for elegance.

COMPOSITION

- Nib-widths remain at 5 for the body, but the ascenders and descenders require more space than formal italic, and the loops must be larger than the bowl.

- Once you have examined the examples, turn the page upside down and observe how more options materialize – "b" and "g" have changed into each other, as have "h" and "y", while "l" now provides another option for "j".

PRACTISING THE LETTERFORMS

In the main, flourishes come from ascenders and descenders, although other letters can be flourished by extending their exit stroke at word ends – "r" is the easiest. Plenty of lubrication with ink is a key to success, as well as a smooth nib that will not catch on the paper when making a sweeping mark. Try removing the pen's reservoir if it is restrictive. Make the marks as an arm movement, rather than all in the fingers.

Write the letters at a 45-degree pen angle.

| **d** g, h, k, l | **b** f, h, k, l | **y** g, p | **D** |

1 This is the simplest flourish. Make the usual "a" shape first.

1 For a more complex flourish, start in the same way as for "d" with a hairline stroke. Then complete the letter shape.

1 For a freeform descender, make the main counter shape in the usual way and ensure the descender starts with a straight stroke.

1 This version of "d" only works with speed. Start the "a" shape as usual.

2 Start the tall ascender with a hairline stroke, then pull down and finish with a serif.

2 Make the seamless join then curve round.

2 Continue with a generous sweep, ensuring that you have plenty of ink to lubricate.

2 Ensure the pen is well charged with ink and push upwards and round.

 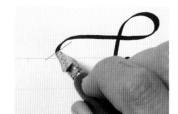  

3 Put the pen back into the upright stroke for a seamless join. Keep the top horizontal, don't allow it to droop.

3 Complete the flourish. With smaller sizes of letter the pen will respond to being pushed, otherwise make the flourish in two strokes.

3 Recharge with ink and make the final stroke with speed to the left and down.

3 Pull across without hesitating and twist as the pen is lifted.

FLOURISHED ITALIC CAPITALS
Lively and informal, these capitals accompany the flourished italic minuscules, or might provide some excitement in an otherwise formal page of writing. They conform to basic italic capital forms, with extensions or freer-flowing elaborating strokes.

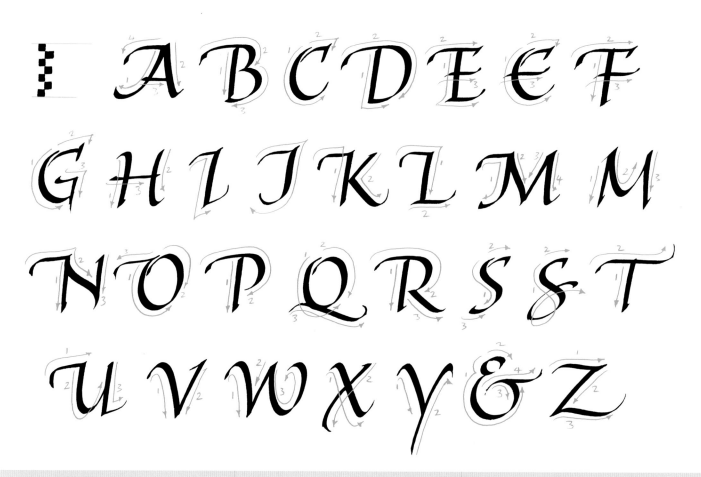

COMPOSITION

- Nib-widths are generally 7 or 8 high, depending on their context.

- Flourished capitals must look convincingly expansive, and not just formal capitals with stuck-on extensions.

- Practical considerations demand that the elaboration occurs to the left of the letter where possible, if minuscules are to follow without an awkward gap.

PRACTISING THE LETTERFORMS

As with the minuscule flourished alphabet, attend to your pen to ensure it flows freely and has sufficient ink to lubricate the rapid strokes. Starting a stroke from left to right is often resisted by the pen, so if you have problems try varying the stroke order, because those indicated are only a guide.

Write the letters at a 30-degree pen angle, except "W".

A M, N	**B** D, E, F, P	**G** C, E, O, Q	**W** V, X

   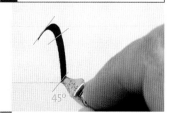

1. Load the pen well with lubricating ink and push in a diagonal stroke down and to the left.

1. Make a strong upright stem with no serifs.

1. To make "O" shapes decorative they can be broken up. Make the first curve.

1. Generously curve the entry stroke but keep the rest of the stroke straight.

2. Complete the second diagonal stroke, then the crossbar.

2. Pull across horizontally, from the flourish to the letter – no drooping – and round to make the top bowl.

2. Pull the second stroke on the side of the nib for a hairline start to the top curve.

2. Keep the second stroke completely straight and overlap it into the corner.

3. Push left and down to complete the extra flourish.

3. Make a larger curve for the bottom bowl.

3. Pull across and down quickly to complete the stem.

3. Make a sweeping curve to complete, or make two strokes if the pen catches, and join up.

VERSALS

Versals, so called because they were originally used in manuscripts as initial letters to indicate the beginning of a new verse, have a long and respected history. Their shape is based on Roman capitals, so it is important to have a grasp of the proportions of that hand before attempting these letters, which are built-up versions.

COMPOSITION

- The thickness of the upright, or stem, is made with two outer strokes and filled in with one more. Thus, the stem is 3 nib-widths wide. The height of the letters is generally 8 stem-widths, and so this will make it 24 nib-widths.
- The pen is held nearly flat – parallel to the writing line – for making vertical strokes, very steep – 70 degrees to the writing line – for horizontals such as in "H", and 90 degrees for vertical fine-lined serifs as in "E" and "F".

PRACTISING THE LETTERFORMS

A steady hand is needed for the vertical strokes, so practise "I" many times, noticing the secret, not exaggerated, swelling at the top and bottom, or "waisting" in the middle. Make the serifs with very fine lines. Next try the horizontal strokes, with the pen held steeply to give a thick stroke but a thin vertical serif. Curved strokes need special care; there is no strict rule about whether you make the inside curve or the outside one first, just make sure the thickest part matches in width with that of the stem.

Write the letters mostly at a 5-degree pen angle.

 L E, F, H, I   **O** G, C, D   **W** V, X, Y, Z   **R** V, X, Y, Z

1 With a flat pen angle, make a fine serif at the top, and two vertical strokes 1 nib-width apart, slightly "waisted" at the middle.

1 Holding the pen at a flat angle, make the left curve and then the right curve, describing the circle, with slightly flattened sides.

1 Make the first diagonal strokes and the fine serif with the pen at a flat angle.

1 Make the upright, "waisted" stem strokes, with a finishing base serif.

2 Hold the pen about 20 degrees from the baseline to make the horizontal stroke.

2 Add the outer strokes 1 nib-width apart, or the inner strokes if the first curves turned out rather wide.

2 Keep the pen flat for the right-hand diagonal in both "Vs", to maintain some thickness, but keep the serifs thin.

2 Including a serif at the top, sweep around to describe the inner curve of "P" or "R", then add the outer curve 1 nib-width away.

3 Fill in the third stroke to make it solid, and turn the pen sideways to thicken the horizontal. Complete the serif and fill in the stroke.

3 Fill in the gap with one more pen thickness.

3 Make the stems solid by the third filling-in stroke, and complete by solidifying the last serif.

3 Fill in the strokes and add the leg to complete the "R".

EDGED BRUSH WRITING

The brush has the ability to be manipulated and twisted to a far greater degree than can a pen, thus achieving subtle "waisting" along the stem strokes, classic serifs and gentle swelling at ends of letters. It is important to hold the brush much more steeply than a pen. In Roman times, lettering for incising on stone was first written with a broad brush. This alphabet is a simplified and heavier-weight version of its Roman ancestor, of which the most famous example is the inscription on the Trajan Column in Rome.

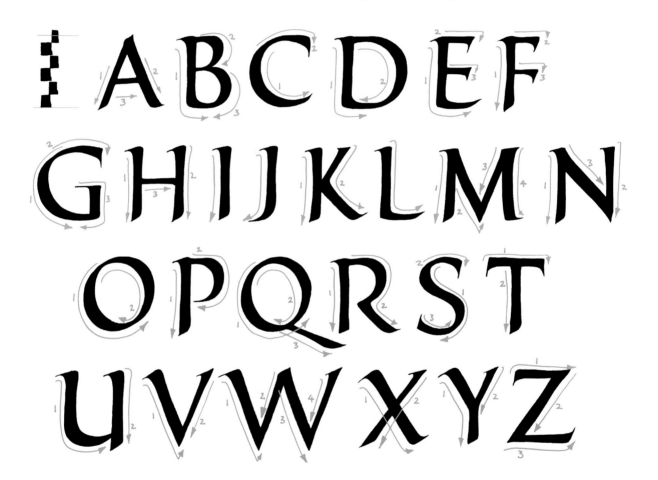

COMPOSITION

■ You will find that the brush's working width is more variable than the pen, depending on how watery the paint, and how well wiped the brush.

■ Precision of brush-widths can only be approximate.

■ This example keeps the letters at a chunky weight of 5½ brush-widths.

■ These letters are also worth exploring at just 3 or 4 brush-widths high, giving informal, solid letters with much presence.

PRACTISING THE LETTERFORMS

Unlike pen-made Roman capitals, these demonstrations concentrate on groups of similar brush strokes, rather than relative widths. It would be helpful to have some background knowledge of the pen-made version before trying these. Strokes are always intended to blend into one another, so try constantly to start or end a second or subsequent stroke well within the existing structure. Watch the many changes of angle that indicate twisting of the brush.

Write the letters mostly at a 30-degree brush angle, but with much manipulation.

E L, F, J, T	**R** I, H, B, P, D	**G** C, O, Q, S, U	**X** A, V, W, Y, Z, K, M, N

1 Make an L first: start the serif with a slight sideways movement, then head downwards.	**1** As with the L, start with a serif then twist downwards for the stroke, thickening up towards the base.	**1** Just below the top line, make a smooth sweep like a half moon, ending in a point.	**1** Start the diagonal with a serif then twist the brush for a steeper angle to avoid too thick a stroke.

2 Start well inside the first stroke, at about 30 degrees, pull horizontally, then twist to make the serif.	**2** Start the curve within the stem, twisting as you follow the curve.	**2** Make a seamless join by starting well within the first stroke, flatten, then twist to make the serif.	**2** Flatten out again to complete the exit stroke.

3 Position the brush to sit just above, not astride, the halfway point of the stem, and repeat.	**3** Twist the brush to an unnatural angle for a pen as shown.	**3** Make the starter stroke of L, but with a flatter serif, and blend at the bottom by heading left.	**3** A flatter angle for this diagonal; make it cross just above the halfway point.

FREEFORM

This lettering is very contemporary, but is based on the italic hand. It could be written with any kind of tool that allows swift, gestural strokes and that makes thin and thick marks depending on how the tool is held. A ruling pen, the kind used in technical drawing for ruling thin lines, is ideal.

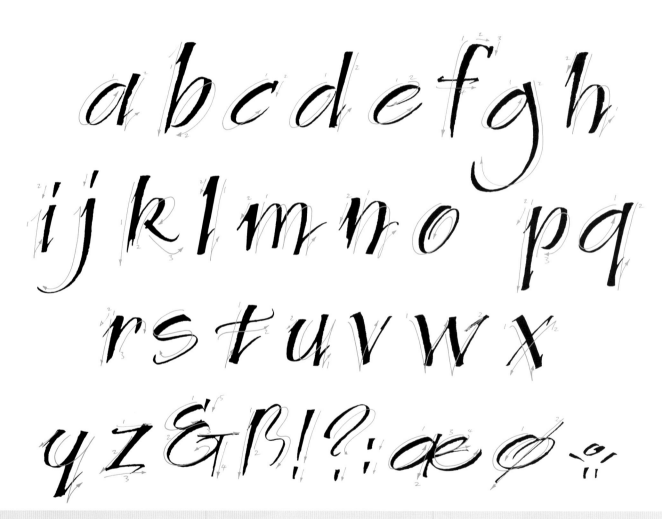

COMPOSITION

■ Nib-widths do not feature when using a ruling pen, because the thickness of the stroke is determined by whether you hold it perpendicular to the paper, using just the point, to achieve a fine line, or on its side, exposing the ink reservoir and discharging more ink in a wider mark.

■ The letters are made with quick, free movements. The pen is held at different angles and twisted high or low on the page to control the amount of ink released. With practice, similar results can be obtained using a nylon pointed brush.

PRACTISING THE LETTERFORMS

The first stroke of the "a" is the most significant shape, and requires practice to get it looking confident and elegant, after which the other letters follow a similar pattern. The "m" and "n" have that same curve, but the other way up. The greatest difference from other scripts is the way you hold the tool, varying the grasp with the fingers, and changing the angles to let out more or less ink.

Focus more on twisting the tool, and ignore traditional pen angles.

| d, g, q | u | h, n, p | w v, x, z |

1 Hold the ruling pen flat to the paper and make a sweeping stroke.

1 Make a similar start as for "a", but with a more open first curve.

1 Use the pointed end only for the upward starting stroke, or leave this until the end as with "y", then flatten the pen against the paper for the thick downstroke.

1 Use the pen flat against the paper at what feels like an unnatural attitude for this downstroke.

2 Twist the pen between finger and thumb so less ink is let out as you complete the upward curve.

2 Replenish with ink and make the downstroke with the pen flat against the paper, flicking up at the end.

2 Twist the ruling pen between finger and thumb to reduce the ink flow for the upward branching stroke.

2 Twist the pen between finger and thumb to reduce the ink flow for the upstroke.

3 Refill with ink and make a thick downward stroke with the pen letting out plenty of ink.

3 Go back to the first stroke and add an outward flick – this is easier than starting with that stroke.

3 Complete the "m" curves by alternately twisting and flattening the pen to produce thick and thin marks.

3 Repeat the pattern in the second "v", finishing with a downward flick.

PART FOUR

ILLUMINATION

ILLUMINATION IS THE DECORATION OF MANUSCRIPTS OR BOOKS WITH
GOLD AND OTHER PRECIOUS METALS, AND COLOUR. EARLY MANUSCRIPTS
WERE WRITTEN IN INK IN CONTINUOUS LINES OF WRITING, WITH LITTLE OR
NO PUNCTUATION TO DIVIDE DIFFERENT AREAS OF TEXT. COLOUR WAS USED
IN THE MANUSCRIPTS TO ENABLE THE READER TO UNDERSTAND THE TEXT
AND TO MAKE THE WRITTEN WORD MORE INTERESTING. SPECIAL DAYS IN
THE CHURCH CALENDAR WERE MARKED BY RED LETTERS, AND FOLLOWING
THE DEVELOPMENT OF MINUSCULES (LOWERCASE LETTERS), CHAPTERS,
VERSES AND PARAGRAPHS WERE WRITTEN WITH A DECORATED AND
ILLUMINATED UPPERCASE LETTER, GIVING EASY ACCESS TO INDIVIDUAL
AREAS OF THE LATIN SCRIPT.

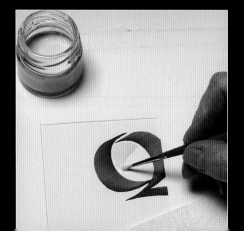
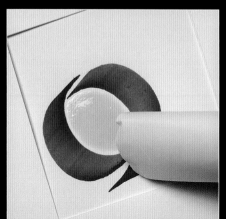

DESIGNING AN ILLUMINATED LETTER There are many ways to

source design ideas, such as studying historical, design and pattern books, visiting museums, exploring the design possibilities of other crafts such as tapestry, weaving and embroidery, or using natural objects, plants and animals as inspiration, in fact anything that stimulates your artistic eye. Here a letter "O" is decorated and illuminated, illustrating the easiest method of applying a design.

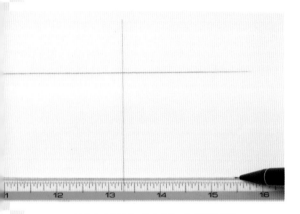

TRACING YOUR LETTER

1 Draw two lines on the back of some tracing paper to mark the guidelines for the letter. Turn the tracing paper over.

3 Draw a centre line, then fold the tracing paper and trace the second half.

4 Alternatively, you can use a second piece of tracing paper to transfer both halves. This way the two sides of the "O" will match.

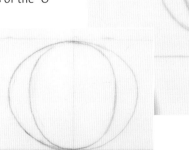

2 When drawing this letter between the lines on the tracing paper, carefully draw one side first.

ADDING DESIGN DETAILS

5 Using several small pieces of tracing paper, draw and trace various design ideas that could fit into the centre of the letter.

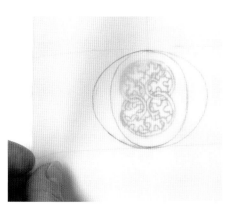

6 Combine the designs with the letter shape by placing them on top of or underneath the traced letter. This enables you to see which designs you prefer. By moving the motifs around many variations can be made, and several pieces of tracing paper can be piled on top of one another to make a composite design or picture.

7 When you are satisfied with the result, tape the pieces of tracing paper together, being careful not to alter the position of the pieces. Place one large sheet of tracing paper over the top of all the pieces.

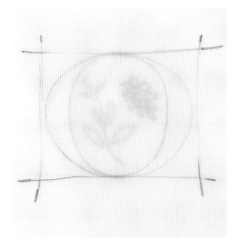

FRAMING THE LETTER

8 The whole design can be placed in a hand-drawn box to add interest. Try this out on the tracing paper to see if you like the idea.

9 Trace the completed design carefully with a 2H pencil. The separate tracings can be saved for another time to make further designs. Tape the new tracing onto watercolour paper with two tape hinges at the top. Prepare a carbon by scribbling with an HB pencil onto tracing paper and rubbing the excess graphite away with a piece of waste paper. Slide the carbon, pencilled-side down, underneath the hinged tracing. Using a sharp 2H pencil, trace down the design.

10 Paint on gesso or PVA where the gold is to be placed and gild the letter (see pages 64 and 68). Paint the design using gouache paint and a No. oo sable or synthetic pointed brush. You may choose bright or subdued colours.

APPLYING GOLD

Gold has three unique qualities: it does not tarnish but retains its brilliance; it can be beaten extremely thin; and it has the quality of being able to stick to itself, so subsequent layers can be added to create the brilliance. Gold needs a size or glue to make it stick to paper or vellum. As these support materials are flexible, the gum also needs to be flexible. Gum ammoniac and plaster-based gesso were the traditional sizes used in the past by historical scriveners and illuminators, and by today's professional illuminators. These gums have been tried and tested for nearly 1,500 years. Gold will also stick to egg white (glair) and rabbit-skin glue, both of which were also used in historical manuscripts.

Modern sizes include acrylic and water varieties, as well as PVA (polyvinyl acetate) medium, also known as craft glue. Shell gold and powdered gold are variations on the traditional gold leaf.

The two techniques of applying gold are known as flat and raised gilding. As the names suggest, flat gilding lays flat to the page, while raised gilding uses a thicker layer of glue to raise the gold from the surface.

Flat gilding.

Raised gilding.

Left: Liesbet Boudens, Opeen Dag. Poem for Bruges, 2002 Cultural Capital of Europe, by Peter Verhelst.

ORDER OF WORK

When using gold it is important to complete any writing first. This is when most of the planning takes place and where mistakes generally occur. All your hard work and time spent gilding and painting will go to waste if a piece has to be discarded because of a writing error. It is also better to apply gold before painting, because gold sticks to everything that is sticky, such as gum arabic contained in paint. Therefore, write first, then apply the gold, and then paint the design.

PAINTING AN ILLUMINATED LETTER

As has already been discussed, paint should not be applied until the rest of the work is done and the gilding is complete and dry. Use a fine artists' No. 1 brush to apply the first gouache colour. Then make further applications of gouache as you build up the design, allowing the previous coat to dry before applying the next and rinsing your brush in clean water each time. The first colour used should be a mid-tone, then add in the shadows (darker colours) and highlights (mixed with white). Add the final highlights in white gouache. This use of tints and shades will give the design form. Try to mix up enough colour to complete each phase in one go, otherwise the shade may vary.

Blue and red were often used together. When one is placed against the other the blue appears bluer and greener and the red very bright. Outlining in black will also make the colours appear brighter. All coloured forms in manuscript illumination can have a brown/black or black outline. Care must be taken not to overdo the white highlighting, otherwise the illustration can appear too busy.

Above: Spring, Summer, Autumn, Winter, by Lorna Bambury. Raised gold, shell gold and gouache on vellum.
Far left: Finished illuminated letter "Q" from page 69.
Left: Completed illuminated letter "O" from page 61.

RAISED GILDING WITH MODERN MATERIALS Raised gilding
can be achieved using a modern medium made from polyvinyl acetate (PVA) or craft glue, which is available from craft stores. It works well on paper but do not use it on vellum or skin.

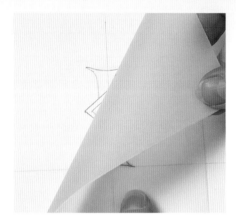

1 Trace your design onto 140 lb (300gsm) hot-pressed watercolour paper.

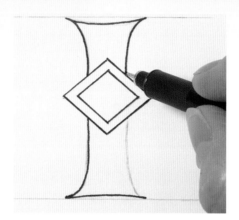

2 Outline the drawing with a dip pen and India ink or a technical pen. Cover the rest of your work with a protective sheet of paper to keep it clean, leaving only the design area exposed.

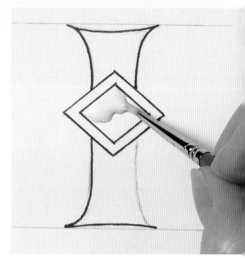

3 Using a No. 0 synthetic brush lay a blob of PVA glue (diluted or not) and gently pull it along the area to be sized. Resist the urge to "paint" it in small strokes, which will cause streaking and grooves. Move the blob quickly and add further PVA blobs as you work.

4 For the serifs or fine endings to letters, place a blob of PVA close to the end and tease the medium outwards. The medium is already drying, so do not retouch any unsatisfactory areas since this will make grooves. Leave to dry for 30 minutes and give the area a second application if you have used it diluted. Always let the previous layer of PVA dry before adding more.

You will need

- 140 lb (300gsm) hot-pressed watercolour paper
- Tracing paper and pencil
- Dip pen with India ink or technical pen
- No. 0 or 00 synthetic brush
- PVA medium and distilled water
- Glass sheet
- Paper
- Transfer gold leaf
- Silk square
- Soft brush
- Glassine (crystal parchment) paper
- Agate burnisher

APPLYING PVA

PVA medium can be applied either by building up several layers of thin medium, or by using one coat of thick medium. For the first method, dilute the medium with 50 percent distilled water, and allow a drying time of 30 minutes between each application. For the one-coat method, the medium should be like thick cream and may only require a small amount of water for dilution.

When dry, PVA medium is transparent, so it is a good idea to add a small amount of red watercolour to the medium to turn it pink, making it easy to see where you are painting and where it is when dry.

Make sure you have all your materials close at hand before you begin.

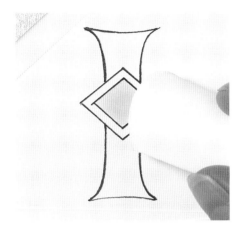

5 When the medium is dry, lay the work on a glass sheet. This helps to condense the warm breath. Using a small paper tube, breathe onto the PVA twice with two deep breaths. This makes it sticky.

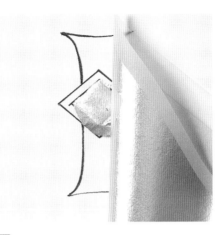

7 Lift the sheet to ensure the gold has stuck. Repeat Steps 5–7 until the whole area is covered with gold.

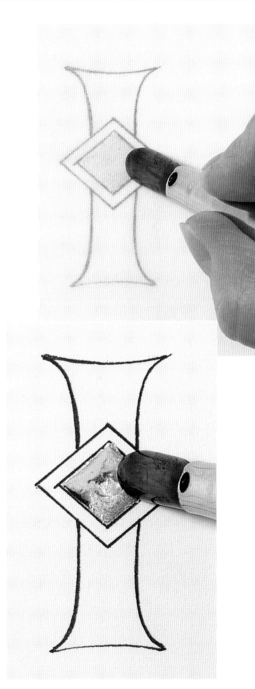

6 Lay the transfer gold leaf, gold-face down, on the sized area and press firmly through the backing sheet with your fingers.

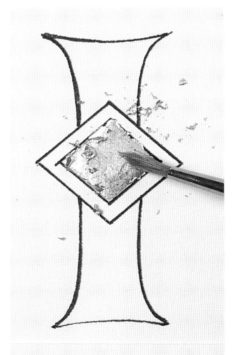

8 Brush away the excess gold and polish gently with a square of silk. Leave for 12 hours to ensure that the medium is fully dry.

9 Cover the gilding with glassine paper and burnish with an agate burnisher (top). Burnish again directly onto the gold for a brilliant shine (above).

FLAT GILDING WITH MODERN MATERIALS The modern materials

you can use for flat gilding include acrylic gold medium, water gold sizes (glues) and PVA medium (craft glue) for
adhering gold leaf to paper or vellum. Shell and other powdered forms of gold and silver require gum arabic.

LEAF GILDING

Acrylic gloss medium and water gold sizes
are ideal gums with which to write, and
the gilding shines brilliantly. For large
areas they are not so successful since they
are difficult to apply evenly. PVA medium
or craft glue can be used to produce a flat
shiny surface of gold on paper by using a
50:50 ratio mix of gum to distilled water.
Large areas can be successfully painted
using thin PVA, making it ideal for flat
gilded backgrounds.

It is a good idea to add a small amount
of red watercolour to whichever glue you
choose to turn it pink. This makes it easy
to see where it has been applied.

You will need

■ Paper
■ Synthetic brush or dip pen
■ Size: either acrylic or water gold size, or
  PVA medium and distilled water (50:50)
■ Transfer gold leaf
■ Soft brush
■ Glassine (crystal parchment) paper
■ Agate burnisher

1 First form your pen-written letter.
Here we are going to gild a background.
Cover the rest of your work with a
protective sheet of paper to keep it clean,
leaving only the design area exposed.

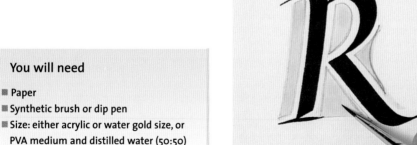

2 Use a synthetic brush or dip pen to
paint on the size. Do not retouch any
unsatisfactory areas since this will make
grooves. Leave to dry for 30 minutes.

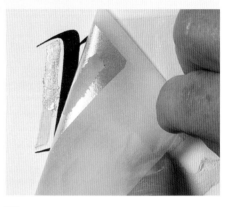

3 When the medium is dry, roll some
paper into a tube. Breathe through the
paper tube onto the size twice with two
deep breaths. This makes it sticky. Lay the
transfer gold face down on the sized area
and press firmly through the backing
sheet with your fingers. Lift the sheet to
ensure the gold has stuck. Repeat until
the whole area is covered with gold.

4 Brush away the excess gold. Leave for
12 hours to ensure that the medium is
fully dry. Cover the gilding with glassine
paper and burnish with a burnisher.
Burnish again directly onto the gold.

POWDERED OR SHELL GOLD GILDING

Backgrounds, small filigree patterns and fine painting can be gilded using shell or powdered gold. The gilding can also be burnished, although the finish is rather dull. Powdered and shell gold can be used on both paper and vellum.

Shell gold is real gold powder mixed with gum arabic, available in tablet form. Use an artists' brush to wet the tablet with distilled water, then apply the shell gold like paint. When it is dry it can be lightly burnished with an agate burnisher.

Powdered gold is real gold powder without the gum, so it needs to be mixed with gum arabic, after which it can be painted on in the same way as shell gold. Powdered gold is sold by the gram. Place 0.5g of powdered gold in a small opaque pot with a lid, such as a film canister, and add 20 drops, using an eyedropper, of gum arabic and just enough distilled water to mix to a thick cream. Once mixed, fill the pot with water, replace the lid, and leave to stand for 12 hours. Decant the water into a second similar pot, keeping the gold at the bottom barely covered with water. The second pot can be kept for replenishing the first with water as it dries out. It can also be used to rinse the gold particles from your brush when you are painting.

2 Gold gouache is applied easily with a fine artists' brush and can produce good flat colour that can be built up and burnished. The gold colour, however, is a little dull and brown.

1 Shell gold produces a good flat surface of gold on a larger area. Drop a small amount of distilled water onto the tablet of gold. Using a fine No. 00 artists' brush, paint the gold evenly inside the letter. Rinse the brush in a small pot of distilled water, keeping the rinsed-out gold for another time. Apply a second coat when dry and burnish carefully.

3 Gold metallic powder is a good and much cheaper substitute for real gold powder. Mix it with a drop of gum arabic to make the resulting paint stick to the paper in the same way as powdered gold. Metallic powder shines very well but is a little textured in appearance. Metallic powders are also available in silver and bronze colours.

RAISED GILDING WITH GESSO
Gesso can be used on vellum and paper and provides a raised "cushion" and ultimately a hard smooth surface on which to apply gold. Once applied to the support and dried, gesso can be reactivated by breathing on it, which makes it slightly damp and sticky again. Every application of gold on the raised cushion of gesso will improve the shine, making the gilding appear rich and opulent. Gesso can be made in batches and stored in an airtight container to be used at a later date.

Making slaked plaster of Paris

Slaked plaster of Paris is the main ingredient in gesso. You can buy it from specialist craft stores, or make your own. Making your own is easy, if a little laborious, and one batch will last for years if stored in an airtight container.

You will need

- 2 gallons (7l) water
- Plastic bucket
- 1 lb (500g) fine dental plaster
- Large plastic or wooden spoon
- Cheesecloth or fine-weave cloth
- Polythene film or large, shallow plastic container

Pour the water into a plastic bucket and slowly sprinkle the dental plaster into the water, stirring continuously with a spoon to prevent the plaster from settling. Continue stirring for at least another 30 minutes. Leave for 24 hours.

Slowly drain away the water, being careful to retain the plaster. Replace with fresh water and stir for 10 minutes. Repeat for the next six days, then every other day for two weeks. Finally, drain the contents through a fine-weave cloth and spread the now slaked plaster into a shallow plastic tray, or onto polythene. While drying, score the surface to create smaller amounts. Grate the slaked plaster into powder as required.

MAKING GESSO

Use a measuring spoon to accurately apportion the ingredients of the gesso recipe. A level ½ teaspoon (2.5ml) used as a scoop is enough to make a good supply. Count each measure onto paper to enable you to check how many scoops you have for each ingredient.

Thoroughly mix all the dry ingredients together in the mortar first and then add the Armenian bole (or red watercolour). Add the seccotine and a little distilled water (use the eyedropper) and grind well with a pestle until the mixture is smooth and creamy. Use a spoon to deposit 1 in. (25mm) cakes of gesso onto a sheet of polythene film and leave to dry. Store in an airtight plastic container.

This mix should make 16 small cakes. A quarter to half a cake will make one gilded letter.

SAFETY NOTES

Gesso contains white lead carbonate, which is an accumulative poison. Remember never to use the measuring spoons, pestle and mortar, or mixing items you have used with gesso for food. Always wash your hands thoroughly after mixing or reconstituting gesso and before eating or drinking.

You will need

- 8 parts slaked plaster of Paris (see Making slaked plaster of Paris, left). This could be substituted with calcium sulphate dihydrate.
- 3 parts powdered white lead carbonate
- 1 part sugar
- Pinch of Armenian bole, or a touch of red watercolour paint
- 1 part seccotine (fish glue)
- 2 parts distilled water
- Eyedropper
- Mortar and pestle
- Measuring spoon (½ teaspoon)
- Polythene film

Place ½ cake into a small pot. Add two drops of distilled water. Leave to soak for 20 minutes. Add another drop of water if required.

GILDING WITH GESSO

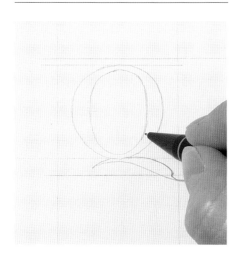

1 Trace your design onto a sheet of 140lb (300gsm) hot-pressed watercolour paper.

You will need

Reconstituting gesso
- Gesso, in the form of a small cake
- Tiny glass jar and lid for gesso
- Eyedropper
- Distilled water
- Glass or plastic rod
- Oil of cloves (optional)

Gilding with gesso
- Tracing paper
- 140 lb (300gsm) hot-pressed watercolour paper
- Synthetic No. 000 brush, or quill or dip pen
- Liquid gesso
- Transfer gold leaf
- Glassine (crystal parchment) paper
- Burnisher
- Smooth agate stone
- Craft knife with curved blade
- Glass sheet

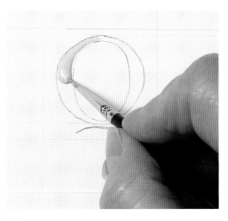

2 Load a fine No. 000 brush, pen or quill with gesso and apply the small blob to the letter. Pull the blob along the letter rather than paint it on because this will cause streaking. Work quickly, carefully teasing the gesso into small areas. Avoid retouching any areas or creating bubbles. Leave to dry overnight.

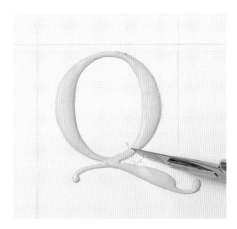

3 Inspect for any rough or uneven areas and scrape smooth with the curved blade of a craft knife or scalpel. Do this with your work on a piece of disposable paper and do not blow any dust into the air. When the surface is smooth burnish with a burnisher (not your best one) or smooth agate stone.

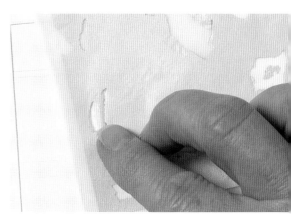

4 Secure your work to a small glass sheet and cover your work with protective paper. Make a small breathing tube and have your patent gold, glassine paper and burnisher at hand. Two deep breaths onto the gesso will revive the medium. Work quickly, laying the patent gold onto the letter. Press it firmly with your finger. Repeat until the whole letter has been covered with gold.

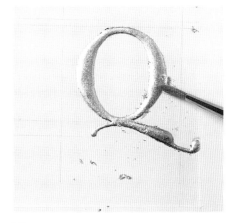

5 Cover the letter with glassine paper and burnish it using your burnisher. A second application of gold will give a brighter shine. Burnish directly onto the gold using your burnisher.

FLAT GILDING WITH GUM AMMONIAC

Gum ammoniac size is made from the milky resin of an African plant. It is simple to prepare and extremely sticky. It flows easily from a pen, which means that you can write with it, lay the gold leaf on top, and create real gold writing. It is ideal for fine filigree decoration and with care it can be laid on large flat areas, either paper or vellum, to create gold backgrounds. It is best not to polish the gold with a burnisher since the heat generated makes the ammoniac glue underneath too sticky. Instead it can be polished with a piece of silk. Gum ammoniac size can be purchased ready-made from a good art supplier, but it is fun to make your own.

MAKING GUM AMMONIAC SIZE

Gum ammoniac is a lumpy substance that looks like granola breakfast cereal. The impurities – debris, seeds, stones – found in with the lumps need to be removed. As a beginner only make a small amount of glue since it does not keep indefinitely.

You will need

- Gum ammoniac in lump form
- Two small glass jars with lids
- Distilled water
- Red watercolour paint
- Fine mesh (or nylon stocking) for straining
- Eyedropper

1 Place about 2 teaspoons of gum ammoniac into a small glass jar. If the lumps are large, break them up a little. Using the eyedropper, barely cover the ammoniac granules with distilled water, stir carefully, then replace the lid and leave overnight.

2 Strain the resulting milky fluid through a fine mesh into another jar, taking care not to push any debris through the mesh. The liquid is the glue. Throw away the mesh containing the bits.

3 Tint the glue pink with a touch of red artists' watercolour paint; this will enable you to see the size. The size can be kept in the lidded jar in a refrigerator for six to nine months. The gum tends to settle on the bottom of the jar after a time, but can be reconstituted by removing the lid, placing the jar in hot water, and giving it a few careful stirs.

APPLYING THE GUM AMMONIAC SIZE AND GOLD

Here we have used gum ammoniac size and gold on 140 lb (300gsm) hot-pressed watercolour paper.

You will need

- Synthetic brush, or a quill or dip pen
- Paper
- Gum ammoniac size (see Making gum ammoniac size, left)
- Glass sheet
- Transfer gold leaf
- Soft brush
- Silk square
- Gouache paints

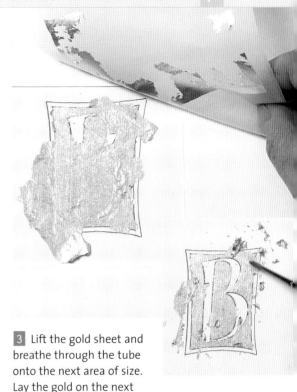

2 Place your work on the cool surface of a sheet of glass. With the transfer gold close to hand, use a paper tube to breathe onto the sized area. The cool surface helps to keep your breath damp as well as warm. Work quickly because the dampness of your breath does not last long. Lay the transfer gold, gold-face down, on the size and press firmly with your fingers. Check the result.

3 Lift the gold sheet and breathe through the tube onto the next area of size. Lay the gold on the next area of glue and rub firmly. When the whole area is covered, use a soft brush to dust away excess leaf and leave until completely dry, preferably overnight.

1 Protect the rest of your work with a sheet of paper. Use a synthetic brush to paint the size carefully but quickly onto the area that you wish to gild. Rinse the brush in warm water as soon as you are finished, otherwise it will be of no use. Alternatively, use a quill or dip pen. Leave to dry for about 20–30 minutes. Secure the lid on the jar to prevent leakage.

WRITING WITH GUM AMMONIAC SIZE

To write with gum ammoniac use a quill or metal dip pen. Keep a small jar of water handy in which to clean the pen now and again, to stop it becoming clogged with gum. Leave the writing to dry, then place the work on a cool glass sheet. Breathe onto the sized writing, press the transfer gold down onto the words until covered with gold. When dry, polish directly with a silk square. The friction caused by burnishing would heat the gum too quickly and spoil the gold.

4 When dry, polish the gold directly with a silk square. Paint with gouache to complete the design.

CELTIC
The most lavishly decorated Celtic manuscripts are to be found between the seventh and ninth centuries, in particular the Book of Kells and the Lindisfarne Gospels. Celtic knotwork, spiral patterns and interlacing adorn the pages and animals, birds and figures are incorporated into the elaborate and complicated geometric designs. To accompany uncial or half-uncial script with a decorative letter it would be useful to study the historical manuscripts written during these times, or some of the many books written on Celtic design.

CELTIC ANGULAR KNOTWORK "A"

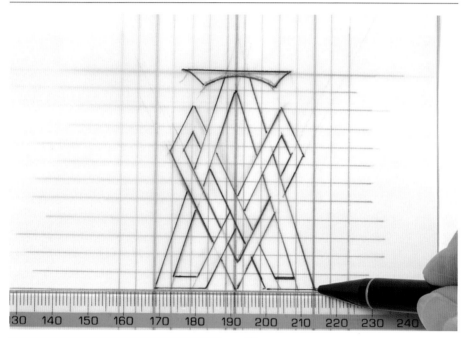

2 Transfer the letter from the tracing paper to 140 lb (300gsm) watercolour paper using a sharp 2H pencil.

You will need

- Tracing paper and 2H pencil
- 140 lb (300gsm) watercolour paper
- Black technical pen
- Artists' brushes: Nos. oo and 1
- Gouache: black; scarlet lake; zinc white; ultramarine blue; green
- Shell gold, or gold gouache
- Burnisher or silk square

1 First trace your design. This Celtic angular knotwork "A" has been adapted from a display capital found in the Book of Kells (folio 183r). It may be useful to make a grid on which to design your letter before tracing.

3 Draw around the design with black technical pen, then fill in the centre of the stems using a No. oo artists' brush and black gouache.

4 Using a No. 00 artists' brush, paint the area shown with shell gold or gold gouache. When the gold is dry it can be polished with a burnisher or a piece of silk. Very little gold was used in the Book of Kells, instead the scribes would have used orpiment (arsenic trisulfide), a highly poisonous yellow that shone like gold.

6 Now add the blue, using ultramarine blue gouache with a touch of zinc white.

7 Finally, add green gouache to the bottom of the letter to complete the design. To enhance the letter further a row of red dots can be placed around the letter, as on the letter "X" on page 74.

BELOW **Many colour combinations can be created for the same design. This "A" features modern colours, with more gold added to the area surrounding the letter.**

5 Using a No. 1 artists' brush, paint the red areas using scarlet lake gouache with a touch of zinc white added. Be careful to leave a gap around the colour. This adds to the brilliance. In historical times this may have been necessary to keep some colours from touching one another, because of the corrosive reaction between them.

SEE ALSO

◎ Designing an
   illuminated letter,
   page 60
◎ Flat gilding with
   modern materials,
   page 66

CELTIC EXAMPLES FOR YOU TO TRACE

Celtic decoration is rich in pattern and colour and the plait, spiral, knot and ribbon motifs can be adapted very easily for modern application. There are also wonderful opportunities to exploit Celtic geometric patterns since endless variations can be built by using grids, circles and dots (see Borders, pages 96–99). For this it will be useful to have a compass, a set square and a ruler. Rubrication, or red dotting, is the first stage in illuminating Celtic letters. It has the effect of making the letters glow by creating a soft tint. These letters can be traced or enlarged on a photocopier.

The script in Celtic manuscripts was from the uncial family of majuscules. Many of the decorative letters shown here are uncial in origin, curved and fluid.

An exuberant pen-written "X" with which to begin a line of uncial or half-uncial writing. One letter extension ends in simple pattern and the whole is surrounded by rubrication.

Celtic "M"

Stylized bird letters can easily be adapted from those found in Celtic manuscripts.

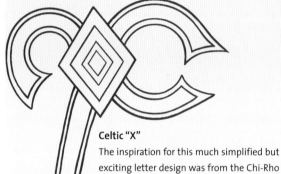

Celtic "X"

The inspiration for this much simplified but exciting letter design was from the Chi-Rho page of St. Matthew's Gospel in the Book of Kells. It may be left modern and plain, or coloured or patterned as you wish.

Celtic "P"

The stylized head of a dog has been made to fit into the bowl of the letter. The design could be used with "D" and other rounded letters. Any colours can be used to decorate the motif.

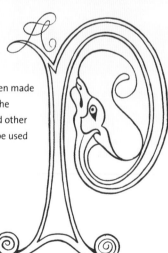

Celtic "H"

This uncial "H" is decorated with a stylized bird. The traditional bright red and blue colours could be used to decorate it, or more modern harmonious combinations could be explored.

An angular display capital with a gold centre.

An angulated capital with a simple but effective knotwork stem and surrounded by red dots.

This simple display capital is similar to those found in the Lindisfarne Gospels. Any colour combinations can be applied when painting.

An angular display capital, adapted and simplified, from the Book of Kells (folio 12r).

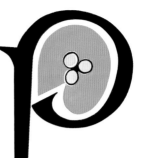

A simple "P" with the stem extended into a lozenge design.

The predominately blue and purple uncial "H" contains simple spiral endings to the letter, and interlacing within the stem.

A simple "M" typical of those from insular Celtic manuscripts. Alternative colours can be used and red dots applied to enhance the outside of the letter.

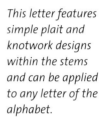

This letter features simple plait and knotwork designs within the stems and can be applied to any letter of the alphabet.

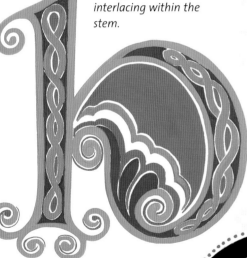

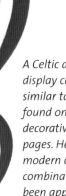

This "M" is copied from a decorative letter in the Book of Kells (folio 309r), with a simple knotwork pattern in both counters of the "M", which could be used within many of the round letters of the alphabet.

A Celtic angular display capital, similar to those found on the very decorative display pages. Here a modern colour combination has been applied.

ROMANESQUE
Romanesque design emerged in Europe during the late eleventh and twelfth centuries. Manuscript art at that time was influenced by earlier Western art – in particular Celtic and Roman – and also modified by Byzantine and Islamic design. The decoration was rich in colour and gold, and the large illuminated initial letters of the display pages were often historiated – containing a narrative scene relating to the text – or inhabited – containing human or animal figures. The borders of the pages also contained figures and animals and much of the decoration was symbolic in nature.

You will need

- Tracing paper and 2H pencil
- 140 lb (300gsm) watercolour paper
- Black technical pen
- Paper cover
- Synthetic brush for gum or size
- Size: PVA, acrylic gloss medium or gum ammoniac size
- Transfer gold leaf
- Glass sheet
- Soft brush
- Glassine (crystal parchment) paper
- Burnisher
- Patent silver leaf
- No. 000 artists' brush
- Gouache: Winsor blue; ultramarine blue; zinc white; scarlet lake

SEE ALSO

- Painting an illuminated letter, page 63
- Flat gilding with modern materials, page 66
- Flat gilding with gum ammoniac, page 70

ROMANESQUE "N"

1 Trace the letter template from page 78 on to 140 lb (300gsm) watercolour paper using a sharp 2H pencil. Draw over the lines with a black technical pen.

2 Cover the rest of the work with protective paper, leaving only the area you are working on exposed. Use a synthetic brush to apply PVA, acrylic gloss medium or gum ammoniac size to the areas of the letter you wish to gild with transfer gold leaf (see pages 66–67 or 72–73). In this example the acanthus leaves will be gilded with silver leaf in Step 5. Leave to dry for 30 minutes.

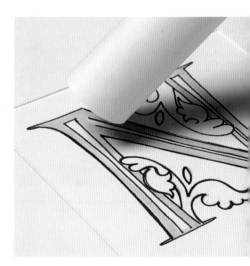

3 Secure the work to a glass sheet, make a small paper tube, and have the transfer gold leaf at hand. Breathe through the paper tube onto the size.

4 Apply the gold face down and press firmly. Continue until the whole letter is covered, then brush away the excess gold with a soft brush. Leave overnight for the size to dry, then burnish through glassine paper before burnishing directly. Brush away the loose particles of gold with a soft brush.

6 Brush away any loose particles of gold and burnish the silver through glassine paper. Then burnish silver directly.

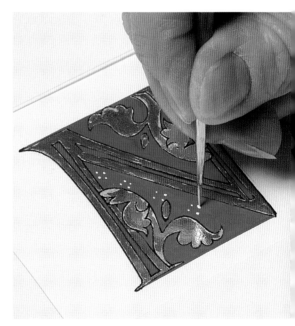

5 Paint the acanthus design with size and leave to dry for 30 minutes. Protect the gold with glassine paper, breathe onto the gum, and press down the patent silver leaf. Silver will not stick to itself like gold does, so must be laid in a single layer – you may want to practise on spare paper first. Silver will tarnish in time adding interesting effects.

7 Paint the blue areas with a gouache mix of Winsor blue and ultramarine blue with a touch of zinc white, using a No. 000 artists' brush. Paint the red areas inside the letter stem with scarlet lake gouache.

8 Further simple patterns can be added to the background with fine white or red dots.

ROMANESQUE EXAMPLES FOR YOU TO TRACE

The manuscripts of the Romanesque period consist of a wealth of initials containing acanthus foliage with stylized fronds and coiling tendrils. The illumination in the large manuscripts was lavish, consisting of display pages and large initial letters with gold and silver decoration. Though most of the manuscripts of this period were ecclesiastical, books for scholars were also being produced.

Romanesque "L"

Black Line "L" adapted from the incipit page of a German Gospel Book from the Benedictine Abbey of Helmarshausen, c.1120–1140. It shows spiralling interlacing vines, which have been executed in gold and silver on a blue and green background.

A modern interpretation of twelfth-century "C", with interlacing vines. Make sure that the intertwining stems look as though they really do grow from one another. The application of green gouache instead of the historical blue and red makes this letter look more modern.

Romanesque "C"

This Black Line drawing has Celtic interlacing on the letter and vines springing from the "C" into the letter counterspace.

Romanesque "Q"

A Black-Line "inhabited" letter – containing a human figure – drawn in English mid-twelfth-century style.

Romanesque "N"

A simplified twelfth-century-style letter, with acanthus leaves curving around the letter stems. The background colours were often divided into red, blue and green in order of colour importance.

This letter has been adapted from a mid-twelfth-century medieval "E". This can be done with most letters of the alphabet, using the fundamental characteristics of historical design.

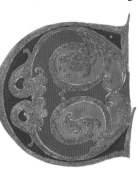

Painted with gold gouache, this letter appears more modern. Altering the more traditional medieval colours of red, blue and green will change it yet again.

This delicate versal has been "modernized" by using flat gold and complementary colours for the decoration.

This letter is adapted from the Floreffe Bible, c.1156. This was one of the display letters from the introduction of St. John's Gospel.

English Romanesque initial "Q" from a late twelfth-century Psalter (Ms, Auct D.2.8). On the original the outer circle is grey, the inner circle green, and the centre square is orange.

An "arabesque" initial letter has ornamentation of fine, linear foliate designs derived from Islamic art. The pen-drawn versal in two contrasting colours is typical of those found in the manuscripts of France and England in the late twelfth century.

A late twelfth-century versal in contrasting colours has been drawn with a pen and filled with paint.

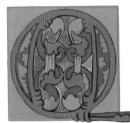

A fanciful pen-drawn versal in red, adapted from those found in the Winchester Bible, England 1160–1175.

This elegant pen-drawn versal is typical of those of the late twelfth century, which were usually drawn in red, blue or green with the flourishing in a contrasting colour. Here a small amount of gold has been added to make it more interesting.

Here is a pen-drawn uncial typical of the twelfth-century English letters and using two contrasting colours with flourished plant-like tendrils. The stem has added white dots for decorative effect.

Letter "Q" adapted from a copy of Gratian's Decretum, France, c.1140, which became the most important law book of the twelfth century.

GOTHIC

The gold on illuminated manuscripts used to be placed onto raised gesso, but today's illuminators have glues, such as PVA medium, at their disposal. PVA medium can be applied in two ways: either in several thin coats, allowing each to dry before the next application, or in one thick coat. To apply thinly, add water until the PVA is like thin cream. The one-coat method requires the PVA to resemble thick cream.

GOTHIC LETTER "U"

1 Trace your design using a 2H pencil. The Gothic letter "U" used in this project has been adapted from a design in the Salvin Book of Hours, a lavishly decorated and illuminated book produced about AD 1270 (thirteenth century).

You will need

- 140 lb (300gsm) hot-pressed watercolour paper
- Tracing paper and a 2H pencil
- No. 000 artists' brush and No. 000 synthetic brush
- PVA medium
- Small paper tube
- Transfer gold leaf and a burnisher
- Scalpel or craft knife with a round blade
- Gouache: ultramarine; Winsor blue; zinc white; permanent white; cadmium red; alizarin red; Winsor green; Havana brown or burnt sienna; black; oxide of chromium

2 With a small synthetic No. 000 brush, paint the background areas that are to be gilded with PVA. Leave to dry for 30 minutes. Use this time to prepare all required tools and materials so they are close at hand. You will need to work fairly quickly.

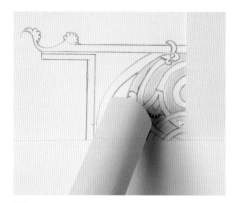

3 Breathe twice through the small paper tube onto the PVA to dampen and warm the glue. This will make the gold stick to the design.

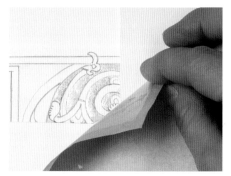

4 Place your transfer gold, face down, onto the PVA design area and press gently with the fingers. Lift to see if the gold has stuck to the PVA. If not, place the transfer gold on the design again and apply more pressure to ensure that it sticks well. Repeat Steps 3 and 4 until no more gold comes away from the transfer.

5 Brush away the excess gold particles. Leave until the glue has dried completely, usually the following day. Trim away any rough edges with a craft knife.

6 Polish the gold lightly with a burnisher. Apply pressure gradually and burnish until it shines well.

7 Mix enough gouache paint to cover all of the blue areas. It is better to mix too much than too little, as the colour is very hard to match on remixing. Paint the blue areas with a mixture of ultramarine blue and Winsor (phthalo) blue with a little zinc white added. Use fine brush, No. 000.

8 Paint the red areas inside the letter with red gouache, using a mix of cadmium red and alizarin red with a small amount of zinc white. Paint all of the green areas with a mix of Winsor green with a small touch of oxide of chromium.

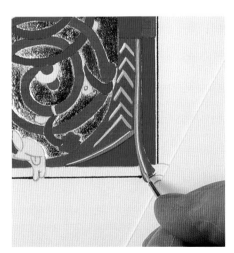

9 Add the white highlighting to the stem of the letter with permanent white gouache using a No. 000 brush.

10 Outline the letter and the design in black or, better still, a mix of Havana brown (or burnt sienna) and black. This makes the colours in the design appear brighter. Outline the box with a mix of Havana brown and black.

11 The finished letter. Add further highlighting in permanent white gouache. This gives the letter and design a three-dimensional effect.

SEE ALSO

◉ Gothic hands, page 40
◉ Flat gilding with modern materials, page 66

GOTHIC EXAMPLES FOR YOU TO TRACE

These designs are only some of the rich examples that you can find within the pages of manuscript books. You can use many different sources for your design ideas: historical books, manuscript books, design and pattern books, or visit museums. Use tracing paper to draw and copy some design ideas. Many variations using the same designs can be made to look quite different by changing the colours.

Early Gothic "E"

This Black Line "E" was inspired by Early Gothic designs of the late twelfth century. The background could be in raised gold with coloured scrollwork.

The spiral of stylized ivy leaves in the centre of this fourteenth-century illuminated "O" is a pattern style repeated many times in Gothic manuscript designs.

This display capital "O" is copied from the Salvin Book of Hours, AD 1270.

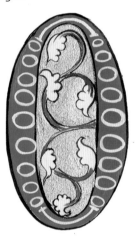

Gothic letter "T"

Adapted from a letter "T" in an early fifteenth-century French Book of Hours, with ivy leaves in red and blue. The letter can be red or blue with a gold background.

This initial "O" is also copied from the Salvin Book of Hours.

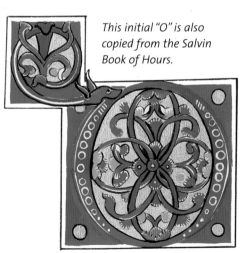

Fourteenth-century "D"

The initial letter "D" in this Black Line drawing is adapted from its position as an integral part of a border design to be found in the Luttrell Psalter.

Gothic letter "O"

This Black Line "O" design was adapted from a thirteenth-century French manuscript. When finished, the colours will be blue and red with a gold background inside the letter.

Inspired by illuminated letters of 1350–1450, this letter "E" contains ivy leaf designs and extended tendrils.

This delicate design has been copied from a small letter found in the Luttrell Psalter c.1340.

The inspiration for this letter "E" comes from late thirteenth-century English illuminated letters.

This pen-drawn Versal "T" in red has contrasting fine filigree pen-work in blue, thirteenth century.

Inspired by the decorative letters found in the Luttrell Psalter of AD 1340, this "T" has a diaper design for the background that is highlighted with white.

Adapted from a French Book of Hours, 1414–1425.

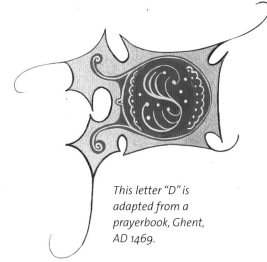

This letter "D" is adapted from a prayerbook, Ghent, AD 1469.

ARTS AND CRAFTS

Much of the work that William Morris created was inspired by his love of nature as a boy, and by studying medieval art, history and manuscripts. These two influences were fundamental to his designs, where leaves – particularly the medieval acanthus leaf – flowers and animals are intertwined and repeated throughout. William Morris was much involved in the Arts and Crafts movement, which was subsequently followed by art nouveau and the graphics and lettering of the early twentieth century.

ARTS AND CRAFTS "T"

1 Trace the line drawing on page 86 and transfer it to a sheet of 140 lb (300gsm) hot-pressed watercolour paper – or vellum as an alternative – using a sharp 2H pencil. Outline the design with a black technical pen or, as here, draw a line with a pen or synthetic brush using permanent green deep gouache with a small amount of black added.

2 Paint the inner area of the letter and four dots in the background with thin PVA glue or gum ammoniac size to give a flat gilded surface that is in keeping with the design. Allow to dry.

3 Breathe onto the letter and apply transfer gold leaf until the size is covered. Finish the gilding by brushing away excess leaf with a soft brush and polishing with a silk square, and burnishing if you have used PVA.

You will need

- Tracing paper and 2H pencil
- 140 lb (300gsm) hot-pressed watercolour paper
- Black technical pen
- Synthetic brush
- PVA glue and distilled water or gum ammoniac size

- Paper
- Transfer gold leaf
- Soft brush
- Silk square
- Glassine (crystal parchment) paper
- Burnisher
- Artists' brushes: Nos. 000 and 1

- Gouache: permanent green deep; cadmium yellow; zinc white; permanent white; Winsor blue

SEE ALSO

- Painting an illuminated letter, page 63
- Flat gilding with modern materials, page 66
- Flat gilding with gum ammoniac, page 70

6 Using the same blue mix, paint the background inside the letter. Add more zinc white to the mix to paint the edges of the petals. Paint the highlighted line around the edges of the flowers using a mix of permanent white with a touch of Winsor blue.

7 Use a No. 1 brush to paint the background colour of the square with permanent green deep. Mix more cadmium yellow and zinc white into the permanent green mix to enable you to paint the highlights on the leaves. Finally, mix cadmium yellow and permanent white gouache to dot the yellow centres of the four blue flowers.

4 With a small No. 000 artists' brush, paint the bars around the gold in permanent green deep gouache.

5 Mix permanent green deep gouache with cadmium yellow and a touch of zinc white to paint the acanthus leaf within the letter. Mix enough of the colour to enable you also to paint the stems and small leaves elsewhere in the design. Mix Winsor blue with zinc white to paint the flowers.

TURN OF THE CENTURY EXAMPLES FOR YOU TO TRACE

There are many wonderful examples of designs created during the last quarter of the nineteenth century and the first quarter of the twentieth century from which to find inspiration. Some of the William Morris designs are reminiscent of not only medieval art but also Gothic and Renaissance letters, particularly White Vine patterns.

Arts and crafts "T"

Black Line drawing of the William Morris inspired "T" used for the project on pages 84–85. The basic letter can be gilded and painted as it was in the project, or adapted to suit your own ideas.

Arts and crafts "U"

Black Line drawing adapted from a William Morris design that was itself adapted from the letters of the Renaissance. This letter could be gilded on a coloured background with white flowers and tendrils. Alternatively, it would look quite different if the background were gilded and the letter painted.

Arts and crafts "A"

A Black Line drawing "A" inspired by William Morris' designs. Colour can be applied to the background and leaves and gold to the outer line of the letter. Alternatively, gold could be applied to the background.

Turn of the century "I"

This Black Line drawing, art nouveau in style, features a simple repeat "tulip" design within the stem of the letter.

This decorated letter is typical of the rounded letter shapes of the art nouveau period, where simple, fluid letters adorned the posters and commercial art of the first half of the twentieth century.

The basic letter design is similar to the turn of the century "T" (left) but with a different plant motif and leaf designs inserted into the letter shape itself.

A gold Roman "T" adapted from a design by Ida Henstock, an illuminator and a working colleague of Grailly Hewitt, both calligraphers of the early twentieth century.

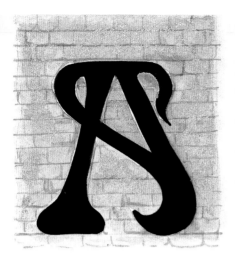

An expressive art nouveau letter from an alphabet by Arnold Bocklin. The style is characterized by soft flowing curves and lines and the absence of geometric design. Transfer gold leaf has been pressed into the background colour.

This "U" is based on a nineteenth-century gilded letter, but has a modern, abstract feel. Only one colour and gold have been used in this design.

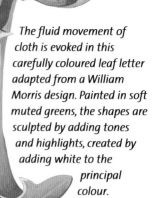

The fluid movement of cloth is evoked in this carefully coloured leaf letter adapted from a William Morris design. Painted in soft muted greens, the shapes are sculpted by adding tones and highlights, created by adding white to the principal colour.

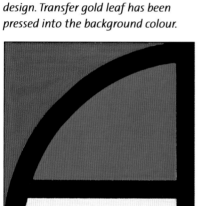

This art deco "A" was simply and effectively drawn with a compass. Painted in flat coordinating colour, it is geometrically very pleasing.

An expressive "A" adapted from those drawn by Alphonse Mucha, whose sensitive and subtle approach to colour and design can be said to be synonymous with art nouveau design.

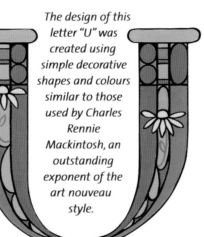

The design of this letter "U" was created using simple decorative shapes and colours similar to those used by Charles Rennie Mackintosh, an outstanding exponent of the art nouveau style.

Similar to the William Morris "I" above, the shape of this letter has been simplified and another mood created with the choice of colours.

A typical Arts and Crafts design adapted from a Renaissance white vine motif, just as William Morris himself did. The green leaves and tendrils travel through and around the gilded letter.

A simple rounded letter similar to those that can be found on the posters of the prolific graphic designer Alphonse Mucha in the early twentieth century.

RENAISSANCE Renaissance is a French term meaning

"rebirth", and applies to the two-hundred-year period from the middle of the fourteenth century through to the mid-sixteenth century. The Italian humanists, in centres like Rome and Florence, used the term when they returned to the classical learning of the Roman Empire. This letter has been inspired by the white, vine-stem design of the early Italian manuscripts, in popular use between 1450 and 1470.

RENAISSANCE "F"

1 Trace the Black Line design from page 90 and transfer it to a small sheet of 140 lb (300gsm) watercolour paper or vellum, using a sharp 2H pencil. Outline the design using a technical pen with brown ink.

You will need

- Tracing paper and 2H pencil
- 140 lb (300gsm) hot-pressed watercolour paper or vellum
- Brown technical pen
- No. 00 synthetic brush
- Gesso (see page 68)
- Craft knife with curved blade
- Burnisher
- Smooth agate stone or old burnisher
- Glass sheet
- Paper tube
- Transfer gold leaf and loose leaf gold
- Soft brush
- Scissors
- Tweezers
- Glassine (crystal parchment) paper
- Artists' brushes: Nos 00–0000
- Gouache: ultramarine blue; Winsor blue; zinc white; scarlet lake, alizarin crimson; Winsor green; lemon yellow; permanent white
- Shell gold or gold gouache

2 Use a synthetic brush to paint the stem of the "F" with gesso, teasing it carefully into the corners of the letter. Create a cushion to give a raised surface for the gold, in keeping with the original manuscript letters (see page 69).

3 Allow 12 hours or overnight for drying, then scrape away any unevenness, lumps or untidy edges with a curved craft knife and burnish with an old burnisher or a smooth agate stone.

4 Secure the work to a glass sheet, make a small paper tube, and have the transfer gold leaf at hand. Cover the rest of the work with protective paper, leaving only the area you are working on exposed. Breathe on the gesso and apply the transfer gold leaf to cover the whole letter (see page 69). Brush away the loose particles of gold with a soft brush.

5 Now apply the loose leaf gold. Gold sticks to gold so there is no need to breathe on the letter again. Open the book of gold holding the spine carefully so the gold does not fall out. Using clean scissors, cut a small square of gold, including the backing paper.

7 Burnish carefully through the glassine paper then directly onto the gold. Cover the whole letter in the same way and brush away any loose particles.

9 For the red areas use a mix of scarlet lake, alizarin crimson and zinc white. Try to create a good balance in the design. Mix the green using Winsor green, lemon yellow and a touch of zinc white and paint the appropriate areas.

6 Pick up the gold and backing paper with clean tweezers or carefully with your fingers, and lay it gently where you require it. Cover it with glassine paper and press firmly on to the letter.

8 Now you are ready to paint with gouache. Mix the blue by using ultramarine blue, Winsor blue and a touch of zinc white and fill in the background.

10 Apply the small white dots on the blue and red areas with a No. 000 brush and permanent white gouache. Add dots of shell gold or gold gouache (see page 67) to the green areas to complete the letter.

SEE ALSO

- Painting an illuminated letter, page 63
- Flat gilding with modern materials, page 66
- Raised gilding with gesso, page 68

RENAISSANCE EXAMPLES FOR YOU TO TRACE

The highly decorative and beautifully illuminated manuscripts of the Renaissance period showed a noticeable concern with realistic interpretation and small miniatures, which were a reflection of the realistic styles of the fresco painters at the time of the Roman Empire.

This raised gilded letter with a painted red gouache background is typical of sixteenth-century decorative capitals.

Renaissance " F"

Black Line drawing of the white vine-stem design of the fifteenth century. This letter can be traced and coloured as illustrated on page 88. Other colours can of course be used.

Renaissance "K"

This Black Line letter is typical of fifteenth-century design.

This three-dimensional letter was copied from the marginal decoration of a French Book of Hours, c.1520, originally made for Francis I of France. His initial letter was incorporated into the elaborate border decoration.

Renaissance "S"

This Black Line letter was inspired by the printed letters of Geoffroy Tory of Paris.

Renaissance "V"

This Black Line letter has been adapted and simplified from a highly decorative manuscript written in Florence in 1488. The beautiful Roman capital was originally executed in raised gold.

This sixteenth-century-style letter has been painted to imitate a classical Roman inscriptional letter, a feature of many of the initial letters of the Renaissance.

This elegant interlacing design can be applied to any letter of the alphabet. It is interesting to note that the vine does not emanate from the letter, as with Romanesque motifs, but only spirals around it.

An example of a late-fifteenth–early-sixteenth century French trompe-l'oeil-style letter, with all the modelling creating a three-dimensional effect. This style of letter is usually placed within a box with a gilded background and decorated with flowers and fruit.

A classical-style sixteenth-century Roman letter painted to look like chiselled stone, accompanied by delicate pen decoration.

This light blue "K" was inspired by an initial letter from a fifteenth-century Bruges Book of Hours.

This design is inspired by the late-fifteenth–early-sixteenth century letters that used sculptured leaves and twig-like stems to create the patterning.

This gilded letter on a raised gesso ground is based on the letters of Florentine manuscripts of the early sixteenth century.

The vine in this white vine-stem motif does not grow from the letter, but twists and curves gracefully around the letter shape as a separate design.

A raised gilded classical letter based on those found in great abundance in the Florentine Books of Hours written in the first half of the sixteenth century. The line decoration can be white or in shell gold.

This letter is copied from the Sforza Hours, from an illustrated and illuminated page by the Milanese illuminator and priest Giovan Pietro Birago working at the end of the fifteenth century.

MODERN

Calligraphy and lettering play a large part in the graphic design industry and the use of exuberant and colourful lettering surrounds us every day. Modern calligraphic and illuminated work can be functional or decorative, subtle or expressive, subdued or outrageous. Today we can adapt letters from a wealth of historical or modern examples and we can manipulate designs and ideas with the use of photocopiers, digital cameras or computers, or we can choose to work with traditional methods and materials to create a variety of letters, words and designs. This letter "H" is based on the uncial letter but appears more modern by the addition of the gold diamond decoration.

SIMPLE LETTER "H"

You will need

- Tracing paper and a 2H pencil
- 140 lb (300gsm) hot-pressed watercolour paper or vellum
- Black technical pen or a ruling pen
- No. 1 artists' brush and No. oo synthetic brush
- A soft brush
- Transfer gold leaf
- Smooth agate burnisher
- Gesso (see page 68)
- Glass sheet
- Paper
- Vellum
- Glassine (crystal parchment) paper
- Craft knife with curved blade
- Gouache: scarlet lake; zinc white; ultramarine blue

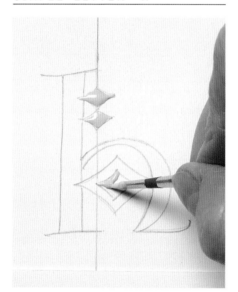

1 Trace the design onto 140 lb (300gsm) hot-pressed watercolour paper or vellum using a 2H pencil. Apply the gesso to the diamonds, using a No. oo synthetic brush, teasing the shapes into fine points. Create a "cushion" for the gold (see pages 68–69). Allow 12 hours for drying, then scrape away any unevenness, lumps or untidy edges with a curved craft knife.

2 Secure the work to a glass sheet, make a small paper tube, and have the transfer gold leaf to hand. Cover the rest of the work with protective paper, leaving only the area you are working on exposed. Breathe twice onto the gesso through the tube and apply the gold face down.

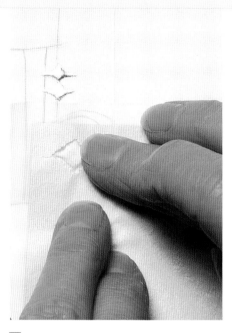

5 Brush away any loose gold with a dry brush and trim any jagged areas with a craft knife.

3 Press down firmly to make the gold stick. Repeat until all the gesso has been gilded.

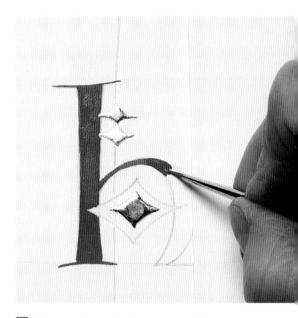

7 Using a No. 1 artists' brush, paint the red letter using scarlet lake gouache with a touch of zinc white added to make it opaque.

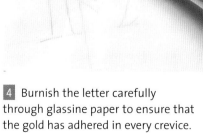

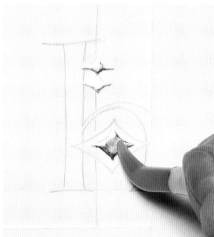

4 Burnish the letter carefully through glassine paper to ensure that the gold has adhered in every crevice.

6 Carefully burnish directly onto the gold to polish it.

8 Paint the diamond edge with ultramarine blue. Finally, draw the red vertical line with a ruling pen filled with scarlet lake gouache, mixed with zinc white.

SEE ALSO

◉ Designing an illuminated letter, page 60
◉ Raised gilding with gesso, page 68

MODERN EXAMPLES FOR YOU TO TRACE

Poetry and prose, words and letters provide the calligrapher and lettering artist with an endless source of inspirational material to express emotion, communicate ideas or invent decorative designs. The variety of letter shapes, related ideas and resulting colour images that can be created is infinite and the moods and feelings suggested are endless. Some of the letters here are exuberant and lively, others are subdued. If you were able to create an alphabet from each of these letters the immediate possibilities are obvious and extremely interesting.

This green italic "B" is written with a manipulated pen stroke. A smaller pen was used for the branches and the gold leaves were created with transfer gold pressed onto painted PVA leaves.

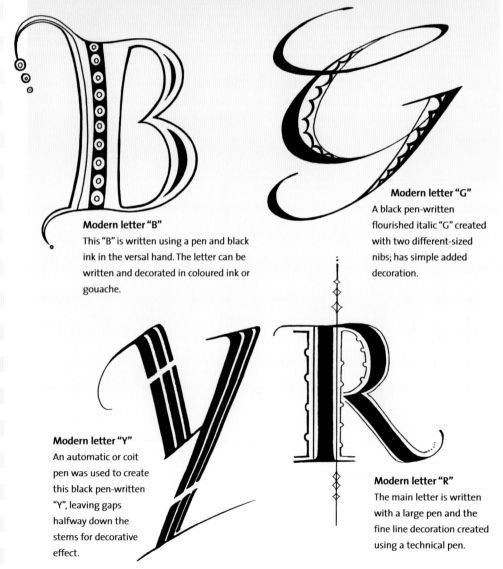

Modern letter "B"
This "B" is written using a pen and black ink in the versal hand. The letter can be written and decorated in coloured ink or gouache.

Modern letter "G"
A black pen-written flourished italic "G" created with two different-sized nibs; has simple added decoration.

Modern letter "Y"
An automatic or coit pen was used to create this black pen-written "Y", leaving gaps halfway down the stems for decorative effect.

Modern letter "R"
The main letter is written with a large pen and the fine line decoration created using a technical pen.

This raised PVA-gilded "B" is surrounded by painted boxes in complementary gouache colours.

An automatic or coit pen dipped in Winsor blue gouache can be used to create this italic letter. The diamond shapes are transfer gold on raised PVA.

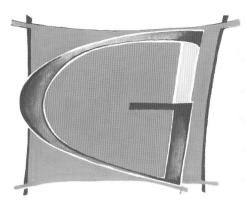

A drawn, modern, formal italic "G" is painted in subtle, harmonious colours for a muted effect.

Written with multiple pen strokes, this freeform "G" benefits from decoration with bright colour, making it appear exuberant and stylish. The gold dots are made with transfer gold leaf on raised PVA.

This foundational letter was written with a pen dipped in thin PVA. A second application was applied using a brush. When dry, transfer gold was applied. The background squares are painted in PVA with silver leaf applied.

A flourished italic letter is written freely in cadmium red gouache and decorated with a smaller nib.

This geometric design was made using a drawing compass and set square, to create a bold and dynamic letter "R".

A pen-written italic capital "R" was traced when dry. The letter was repeated four times to create a design. One was gilded with transfer gold on PVA, while the letters behind were painted.

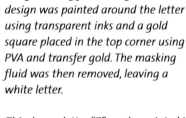

This lowercase "y" was freely written using masking fluid. The geometric design was painted around the letter using transparent inks and a gold square placed in the top corner using PVA and transfer gold. The masking fluid was then removed, leaving a white letter.

This drawn letter "Z" can be painted in gold gouache or gold metallic powder with added gum. The addition of gold dots and a painted background completes the design.

A drawn "Z" painted in metallic copper powder mixed into scarlet red gouache.

BORDERS
The following designs illustrate how easy it is to draw and paint a variety of borders. For your first attempts you can practise with pencil and coloured pencils or watercolour paints, until you are sure of the pattern you wish to design.

FOUR-LINE GRID

To accurately execute the first four borders you will need to draw a grid of squares in the form of strips across the page. Draw a square at the side of the paper, then mark in the top and bottom lines right across the sheet. Divide the square by drawing the diagonals. This will give you the centre horizontal and vertical lines. Divide the small top and bottom square with their diagonals to create two further horizontal lines that are equidistant. Use a 45-degree set square to create the diagonals of each of the following squares across the page and create a perfect four-line grid. Endless different simple or complex patterns can be achieved using a four-line grid.

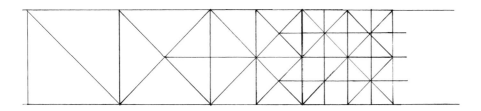

GREEK KEY

This pattern is called a "fret" or "Greek key", and follows the pattern on the four-line grid. This design was sketched first, then painted with gouache.

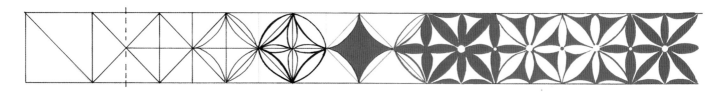

GEOMETRIC FLOWER BORDER

A pattern of simple red and white flowers can be created using the four-line grid. You will find that the flower patterns can be repeated or alternated, and different combinations can be composed with a little concentration.

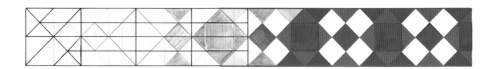

DIAMOND DESIGN

A simple but bold harlequin pattern using Winsor red, Winsor blue and white gouache has been created on this four-line grid.

FLORAL GEOMETRIC

Here the four-line grid has been used to make a more complicated pattern of blocks of colour and flower patterns. Try making a coloured pencil sketch first, to establish how the colours combine best, then paint with gouache. Extra decoration can be added to the design by including white or coloured dots, small circles or square patterns, or painted motifs within the coloured areas.

NATURALISTIC REPETITION

A traced motif has been reversed each time it was repeated to create this border pattern. Draw the line of squares to the desired width and length and, with a pencil, draw the gracefully curving stalk imaginatively through the squares. Add

the motif, carefully reversing the design each time. Add individual leaves and flowers where you feel they are needed to balance the design. A palette of gouache paint featuring Winsor green, lemon yellow and cadmium yellow deep has

been used for the design. Permanent white was used for the dots on the leaf veins. For even more patterning, further small flowers and leaves can be added to the stem. This will make the design appear more complicated.

THISTLE MOTIF

Only half of this thistle design was drawn and traced. The tracing was then reversed to make the pattern. Forest green gouache was mixed with cobalt blue and zinc white for the grey-green leaves and stems, while purple lake was used for the

thistle. Alizarin red was added to the green to make the almost black berries. Artists' watercolour paint would give a softer, more realistic appearance than gouache.

BORDER EXAMPLES FOR YOU TO TRACE

The examples shown here can be used to complement the range of scripts and illuminated letters illustrated in the book. The border designs date from early Celtic and Gothic through to modern interpretations of pattern and contain the characteristics of each era to provide inspiration and stimulate further ideas.

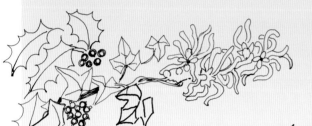

Modern Floral border
This modern border design makes great use of leaves and flowers.

This modern pen and colour border is written with waterproof ink. It could be coloured using watercolour or gouache paint, but keep the paint watery for the best effect.

Traditional Historical border
This typical Gothic border design of the fourteenth century will work well with the illuminated Gothic letters on pages 82–83.

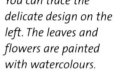

You can trace the delicate design on the left. The leaves and flowers are painted with watercolours.

Arts and Crafts border
This Acanthus border is typical of those created by William Morris at the turn of the twentieth century.

Arts and Crafts border
This ivy leaf and seed pod can be used to create many styles of border. See the next page for ideas.

Random calligraphic marks and freely written letters can make an exciting border. This one uses waterproof ink for the mark-making and coloured inks to create colour. Gold can be added by painting with PVA or acrylic size.

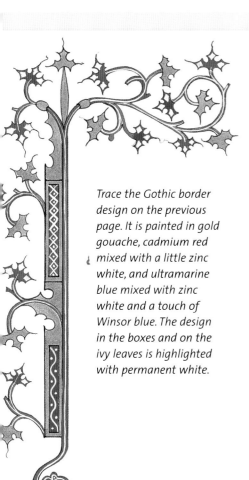

Trace the Gothic border design on the previous page. It is painted in gold gouache, cadmium red mixed with a little zinc white, and ultramarine blue mixed with zinc white and a touch of Winsor blue. The design in the boxes and on the ivy leaves is highlighted with permanent white.

This Arts and Crafts border design can be traced on the previous page. Reverse the design at the corner. The border is painted with watercolours and then gouache paint. Forest green and cadmium yellow have been used to create the greens.

To create the Celtic Knot border, mark dots on either side of parallel lines and join them to create the skeleton shape, then build up their weight. Follow the "over and under" knotwork. To break the pattern, add strands of colour.

The Single Strand Celtic Knot is created using parallel lines, marking them at alternating points to form triangles. Build up the weight and check the "over and under" formation.

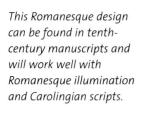

This Romanesque design can be found in tenth-century manuscripts and will work well with Romanesque illumination and Carolingian scripts.

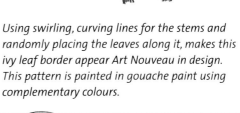

Using swirling, curving lines for the stems and randomly placing the leaves along it, makes this ivy leaf border appear Art Nouveau in design. This pattern is painted in gouache paint using complementary colours.

Yves Leterme
Background detail

Speedball and black ink, background detail. A fine example of "gestural" calligraphy with sensitivity to form, quality of line, and sharpness.

Linda Truyers
Writing on a box, detail

The placing of two contrasting scripts at right angles adds extra visual excitement.

Liesbet Boudens
IDEM, detail

Letterform and counter spaces complement each other, and a simple red square becomes a major feature.

Lin Kerr
The land, detail

Freeform lettering in colour and gold, additionally enlivened with illustrative background (see page 154).

PART FIVE

GALLERY

FEAST YOUR EYES ON THE FOLLOWING PAGES. HERE MANY CALLIGRAPHERS DISPLAY THEIR DIVERSE AND CREATIVE SOLUTIONS FOR PUTTING WORDS ONTO PAPER AND OTHER SURFACES. TO COMPLEMENT EARLIER MATERIAL IN THIS BOOK, WE HAVE LOOSELY GROUPED THE WORKS INTO THREE CATEGORIES: FORMAL ENCOMPASSES RECOGNIZABLE SCRIPTS ARRANGED, GENERALLY, ON STRAIGHT LINES; INFORMAL INDICATES A FREER APPROACH, OFTEN WITH MORE GESTURAL WRITING; AND GILDING EMBRACES ILLUMINATION IN THE TRADITIONAL SENSE AS WELL AS MODERN EXPERIMENTAL USES OF GOLD. SOME WORKS QUALIFY UNDER TWO HEADINGS, SO DO NOT CONFINE YOURSELF TO ONE SECTION IF SEARCHING FOR PARTICULAR INSPIRATION.

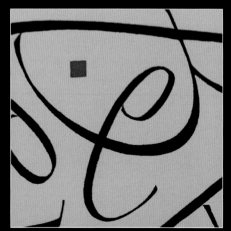

Heleen de Haas
Writing on ceramic torso, right

Calligraphy has more meaning when the medium is also considered, as with this piece inspired by African women's jewellery (see page 119).

Izumi Shiratani
Setzu Getsuka

Bringing together Western freeform writing and oriental calligraphy (see page 125).

Ann Bowen
Raised gold, detail

Raised gold need not always be in the lettering; it can also be used as a decorative feature (see page 137).

Lin Kerr
Nkosi Sikelela Africa, detail

Crossing cultures, combining ancient patterning with modern painterly expression (see page 154).

FORMAL

THE WORK IN THIS SECTION SHOWS THAT "FORMAL" NEED NEVER MEAN
"DULL" OR "PREDICTABLE", BUT NEVERTHELESS OBSERVES ESTABLISHED RULES
FOR BALANCED LAYOUTS, WITH ATTENTION TO SPACING AND MARGINS.
LETTERFORMS REFLECT THEIR CLASSICAL ORIGINS, ALTHOUGH SOME HAVE
MOVED ON TO MODERN VERSIONS.

George Thomson with Miho Hokiyama
Seasonal Japanese verse –
Autumn 2

Uncial lettering. Computer-
aided calligraphy; handwritten
Japanese script on oriental
paper.

AN AUTUMN EVE
SEE THE VALLEY MISTS ARISE
AMONG THE FIR LEAVES
THAT STILL HOLD THE DRIPPING WET
OF THE CHILL DAY'S SUDDEN SHOWER

Leonid Pronenko
The Union of Different Arts

Cyrillic script. Reed broad pen, gouache, paper.

George Thomson
An Uair (When the Ship was Poised)

Gaelic text by Alastair MacDonald 1695–1770. Uncial lettering. Computer-aided calligraphy on Arches mould-made paper.

George Thomson
Of Water Lillie, from *The Herball,*
***or General Historie of Plantes* by**
John Gerard

Uncial titles and italic text.
Computer-aided calligraphy on
Arches mould-made paper.

Janet Mehigan
To the Ends of the Earth

Extract from a Ranulph Fiennes
book. Acrylic ink wash on masking
fluid, gouache versals.

This dwarfe water Lillie differeth not from the other small yellow water Lillie, saving that, that this kinde hath sharper pointed leaves, and the whole plant is altogether lesser. wherein lieth the difference. This hath the floures much lesse than those of the last described, wherefore it is fitly for distinction sake named Nymphaea lutea minor flore parvo.

NYMPHAEA LUTEA MINOR FLORE PARVO

OF WATER LILLIE
OR THE GENERALL

THe white water Lillie or Nenuphar hath great round leaves, in shape of a Buckler, thick, fat, and full of juice, standing upon long round and smooth foot-stalks, ful of spungious substance; which leaves do swim or flote upon the top of the water: upon the end of each stalk groweth one floure onely, of colour white; consisting of many little long sharpe pointed leaves, in the middest whereof bee many yellow threads: after the floure it bringeth forth a round head, in which lieth blackish glittering seed. The roots be thicke, full of knots, blacke without, white and spungie within, out of which groweth a multitude of strings, by which it is fastened in the bottome.

THE EVENINGS WERE SOFT AND FULL OF WILD BEAUTY
WHICH FADED FROM RED DUSK INTO PURPLE DAWN WITH NO NIGHT-TIME BETWEEN
BUT WINTER WAS POISED ON THE BALLS OF ITS FEET   TO THE ENDS OF THE EARTH
RANULPH FIENNES

ALREADY THE SUN AT MIDNIGHT CARESSED THE SILENT SURFACE OF THE SEA

FROM THE HERBALL

HISTORIE OF PLANTES

The Place - These herbes do grow in fennes, standing waters, broad ditches, and in brookes that run slowly, and sometimes in great rivers.
The time - They floure and flourish most of the Sommer moneths.
The Temperature - Both the root and seed of water Lillie have a drying force without biting.

The leaves of the yellow water Lillie be like to the other, yet are they a little longer. The stalkes of the floures and leaves be like: the floures be yellow, consisting onely of five little short leaves something round; in the midst of which groweth a small round head, or button, sharpe towards the point, compassed about with many yellow threds, in which, when it is ripe, lie also glittering seeds, greater than those of the other, and lesser than wheat comes. The roots be thick, long, set with certaine dents, as it were white both within and without, of a spungious substance.

...smal white water Lillie floteth likewise upon the water, having a single root, with some few ...es fastened thereto: from which riseth up many long, round, smooth, and soft foot-stalkes. ...ne of which doe bring forth at the end faire broad round buckler leaves like unto the precedent, ...lesser: on the other foot-stalkes stand prettie which floures, consisting of five small leaves ...ea, having a little yellow in the middle thereof.

YELLOW WATER LILLIE

JOHN GERARD

Nymphaea lutea minor flore pumilo

The small yellow water Lillie hath a little threddie root, creeping at the bottome of the water, and dispersing it self far abroad: from which rise small tender stalkes, smooth and soft. whereon do grow little buckler leaves like the last described: likewise on the other small stalke standeth a tuft of many floures likewise floting upon the water as the others do. This hath the floures larger than those of the next described, wherefore it may be fitly named Nymphaea lutea minor flore amplo.

Veiko Kespersaks
Faith, Prayer

Experimental capitals in gouache on handmade paper.

FAITH OPENS THE DOOR SO THAT THE JOURNEY MAY BEGIN · WILL GIVES THE STRENGTH AND DESIRE TO GO · HOPE GIVES WINGS ·

FAITH WILL KNOWLEDGE HOPE FORGIVENESS LOVE PRAYER

KNOWLEDGE SHOWS THE RIGHT DIRECTION · LOVE GIVES STRENGTH · FORGIVENESS GIVES FREEDOM ·

PRAYER HELPS TO DIRECT THE FLOW OF SPIRITUAL ENERGIES TO FORM A CREATIVE BOND WITH GOD ·

George Thomson
One, Two, Buckle My Shoe

Italic lettering.
Computer-aided
calligraphy on
Auracolor.

1234567890123456789012345678901234567890
one two buckle my shoe
1234567890123456789012345678901234567890
three four knock at the door
1234567890123456789012345678901234567890
five six split up sticks
1234567890123456789012345678901234567890
seven eight lay them straight
1234567890123456789012345678901234567890
nine ten a big fat hen
1234567890123456789012345678901234567890

Mary Noble
Harmony with Nature

Italic capitals in
gouache, with metal
pens, on handmade
Indian Khadi paper,
embossed and tinted.

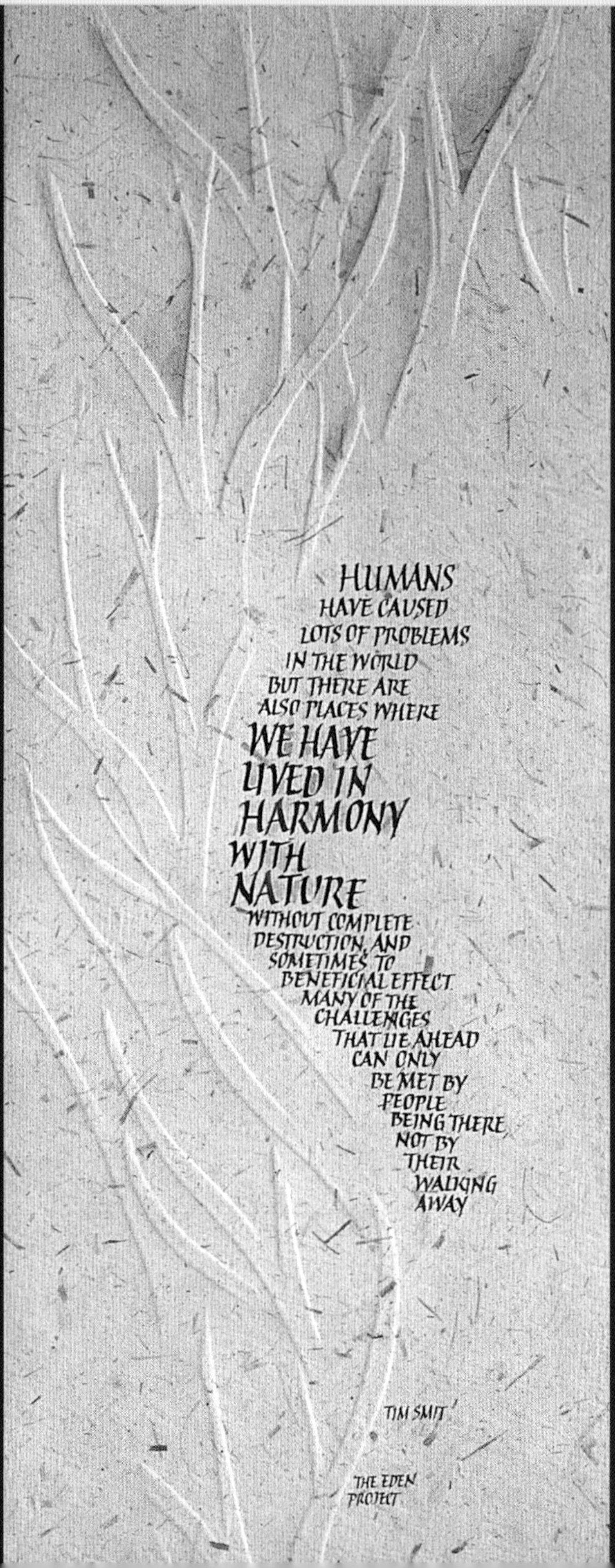

Dominoes

George Thomson
Dominoes

Computer-aided
calligraphy on
Auracolor.

HUMANS
HAVE CAUSED
LOTS OF PROBLEMS
IN THE WORLD
BUT THERE ARE
ALSO PLACES WHERE
WE HAVE
LIVED IN
HARMONY
WITH
NATURE
WITHOUT COMPLETE
DESTRUCTION, AND
SOMETIMES TO
BENEFICIAL EFFECT
MANY OF THE
CHALLENGES
THAT LIE AHEAD
CAN ONLY
BE MET BY
PEOPLE
BEING THERE
NOT BY
THEIR
WALKING
AWAY

TIM SMIT

THE EDEN
PROJECT

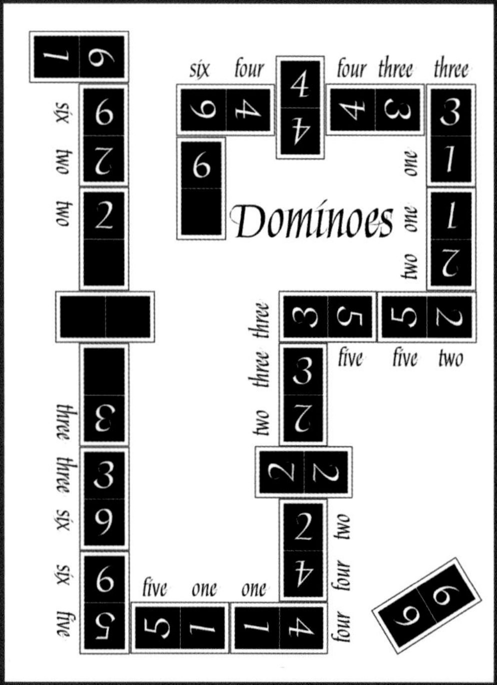

Jan Pickett
Alphabet

Lightweight foundational contrasted with Gothic, using ink, edged pens and soft pencil.

Christopher Haanes
Tyngdekraft (Gravity) by Rainer Maria Rilke

Extract from a poem. An italic form with pen manipulation, using Brause nib, ink on Khadi Indian handmade paper.

Susan Richardson
Let It Be

Capitals turned into regular pattern, written in Sumi ink on a pen on Arches paper.

Christopher Haanes
Hunters Delight . . .

Demonstration piece. Ink on khadi Indian handmade paper, mapping pen, letters built up.

HUNTERS
DELIGHT
ESPECIALLY
IN KILLING
BEAUTY

ERNST JÜNGER

Nadia Hlibka
RA

Chalk, charcoal and gouache on watercolour paper. Drawn Roman capitals, ruling pen lettering background.

Liesbet Boudens
DE TIJD

Drawn and painted capitals. Gouache on Fabriano Roma.

John Neilson
White the

10½ x 15 x ¾ in. (267 x 381 x 19mm). Riven Welsh slate; lettering v-incised; from R. S. Thomas's poem "The Signpost", publisher: J.M. Dent.

Gemma Black
Trajan and versal (detail)

Watercolour painting cut back in around drawn letters in five layers. Watercolour versals, gouache foundationals.

Linda Truyers
The Earth is Full of Heaven

Versal capitals. Acrylic paint on stone.

John Neilson
Snail

40¾ in. (1020mm) tall. St. Bees sandstone. Text by pupils of Stainton Primary School, Cumbria.

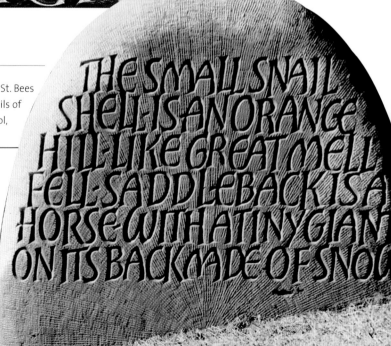

...ENTY SIX
...ETTERS
...H WITH
...VIDUAL
...CTER AND
...RPOSE

of and useful signs but a

BLACK

Letters act as

Mary Noble
American Indian marriage blessing (detail)

Heavyweight Roman capitals, and pointed and freeform italics. Chisel-edged brushes and gouache on calico banner coated with latex paint and rollered Plaka.

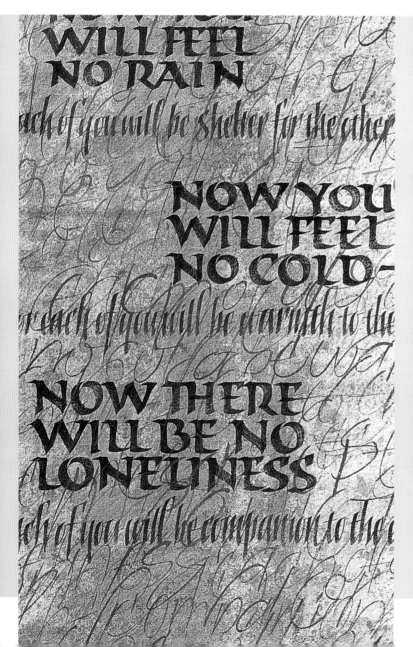

Dona Stenstrom
Women Who Run (Dr. C. Estes)

Handmade paper, found natural objects, sticks, italic lettering in gouache inks.

Gerald Moscato
City Lights

Gothic letters with extensions. Bleach in technical pen and stippled background on black buck-eye paper.

Dona Stenstrom
Enthusiasm

Masking fluid resist, watercolour and ink italics.

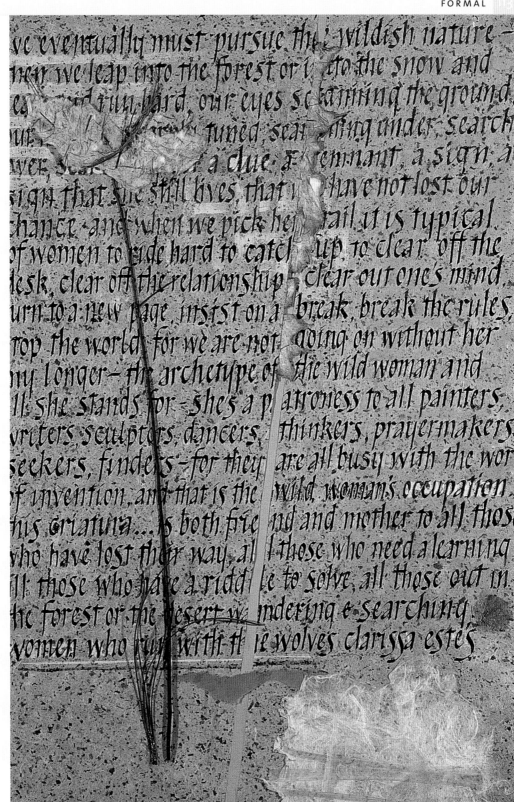

INFORMAL

AN EXPERIMENTAL APPROACH TO LETTERING OR DESIGN CAN TAKE
CALLIGRAPHY INTO NEW WORLDS. SUCCESSFUL EXECUTION DEMANDS A
CLOSE APPRECIATION OF SHAPE AND NEGATIVE SPACE, EQUALLY AS MUCH
AS THAT REQUIRED FOR TRADITIONAL WORKS, YET THEIR FLOWING MARKS
APPEAR EFFORTLESS AND UNCONTRIVED.

An Vanhentenrijk
Verzet by Remco Campert

Compact Roman capitals and
italic-based free lettering. Sumi
ink, bleedproof white, automatic
pen, Brause nib, on paper.

VERZET BEGINT NIET
MET GROTE WOORDEN MAAR MET KLEINE DADEN ZOALS
STORM MET ZACHT GERITSEL IN DE TUIN OF DE KAT
DIE DE KOLDER IN Z'N KOP KRIJGT ... ZOALS BREDE
RIVIEREN MET EEN KLEINE BRON VERSCHOLEN
IN HET WOUD ... ZOALS EEN VUURZEE MET DEZELFDE
LUCIFER DIE DE SIGARET AANSTEEKT ...
ZOALS LIEFDE MET EEN BLIK EEN AANRAKING IETS DAT OPVALT IN EEN STEM
JEZELF EEN VRAAG STELLEN DAARMEE BEGINT VERZET
EN DAN DIE VRAAG
AAN EEN ANDER STELLEN

Ann Bowen
Alphabet

Ruling pen, white and gold gouache freeform italics on BFK Rives.

An Vanhentenrijk
Over de dood heen by Claire Vanden Abbeele

Roman capitals and freeform italic. Sumi ink, walnut ink, bleedproof white, oil pastel, with Brause, ruling and automatic pens, on Steinbach paper.

Lieve Cornil
Rien

Inks, bleach and automatic pen freeform italic capitals on paper.

Lilly Lee with John Rutter
The letter "P"

Created for a Honda 2000 brochure cover. Pen and ink by Lilly Lee. Photoshop manipulation by John Rutter.

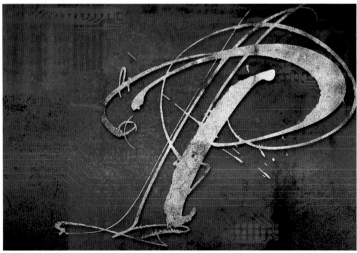

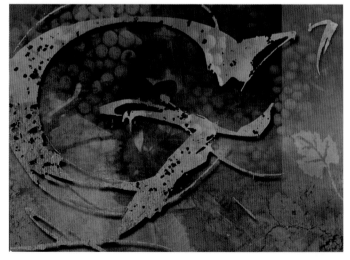

Lilly Lee
The letter "G"

Design and concept inspired by
Napa Wine Auction promotional
cards themed on Penti.

Jill Quillian
Decorated "A"

Paste paper background, coloured pencil
drawing "A", based on a versal capital,
Schmincke gold gouache flourishes.

Heleen De Haas
In die begin

Ceramic vase with freeform
italic lettering, engraved
using Cola pen. Calligraphy
Teaching and Design Studio,
Cape Town RSA.

John Neilson
Canto

48 in. (1220mm) tall. Hopton
Wood limestone. The word
canto is repeated on the back
in the text *En el canto de la
piedra suena el mar.*

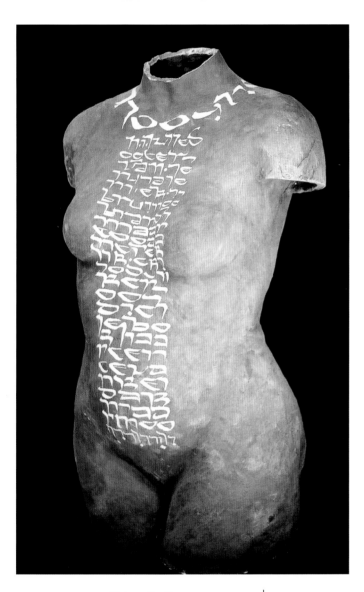

Heleen De Haas
Dogters van Jerusalem

Ceramic torso, black slip engraved with own alphabet design. Resembles jewellery worn by African women.

John Neilson
There Are No Unsacred Places

36 in. (900mm) tall. St. Bees sandstone. Text from poem by Wendell Berry, from *The Gift of Gravity*, publisher: Golgonooza Press.

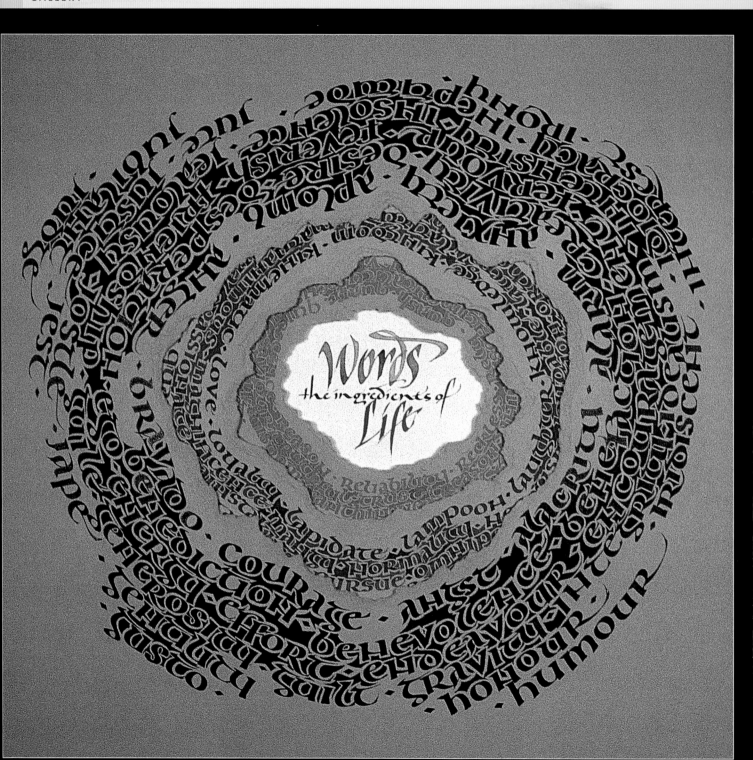

Jan Pickett
Words – the ingredients of life

Centre lettering is based on italic, outer lettering is uncial. Walnut ink on layers of torn BFK Rives paper.

An Vanhentenrijk
Alphabet Expressions 1–2–3

Roman capitals, heavyweight, and freeform italics in Bleedproof White and oil pastels on paper.

Heleen De Haas
As U woord oopgaan

Freeform italic lettering. Gouache, watercolour, graphite, foil and Aquarelle; Cola pen, brush and metal nib.

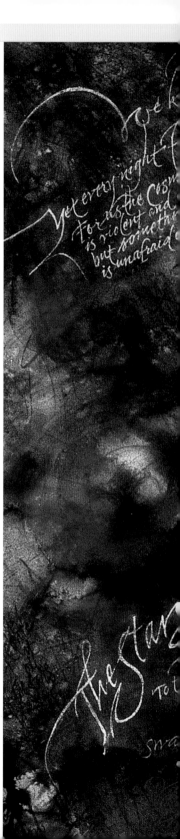

Jenny Hunter Groat
The Stars are History

Watercolour and gouache, gold
leaf flourished italic, pointed
brushes.

Gemma Black
Fire, versal "K"

Watercolour background and
versal, Mitchell nib and fine
rapidograph pen.

Dona Stenstrom
One year is sufficient (detail)

Flourished italic lettering.
Watercolour, ink, gouache and
masking fluid.

some have died, their nuclear fires consumed and dark, leaving only pulsing

aking javelins of light

universe
is not real

the mathematics of the dark

order even chaos

holy flicker

how do we know that we are alive at all

change is not the same as death

history

You are a world breathing in a rock
I am a feathered sun in borrowed earth
and thought, like starlight, startles the receiving mind

Linda Truyers
The Secret by Toon Hermans

Freeform italic lettering. Several layers of walnut, pearl and ecoline inks, Brause pen, white gouache and ruling pen.

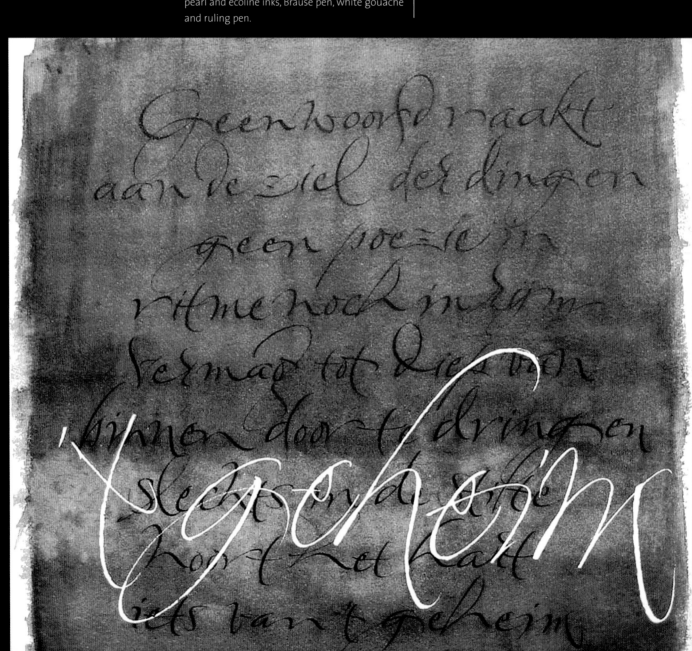

Izumi Shiratani
There's a Divinity

Chinese ink, brush on paper.

Izumi Shiratani
Setsu Getsuka

Japanese and freeform italic. Brush and ruling pen with Chinese ink and gouache across three canvases.

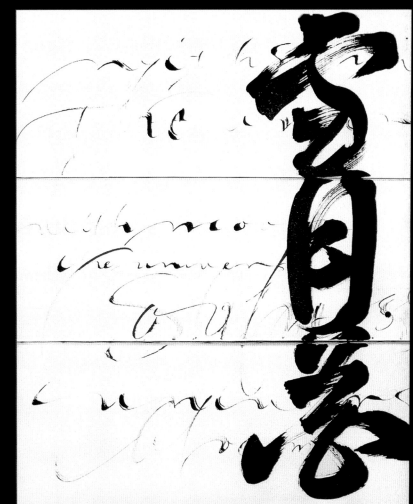

Nadia Hlibka

Variations on a Draft of Shadows (detail)

Italic and built-up versals. Collage and overwritten small squares; charcoal paper; acrylic, gouache, coloured pencil, brush, pointed pen.

Judy Dodds

God at Work, 1 Thessalonians

2003. Client: St. Christopher's Episcopal church. Drawn and written Roman and italic capitals. Watercolours on Arches cold-pressed paper.

Nadia Hlibka

And This Alone?

Built-up double-stroke versals in gouache over acrylic and watercolour background, colour pencil throughout.

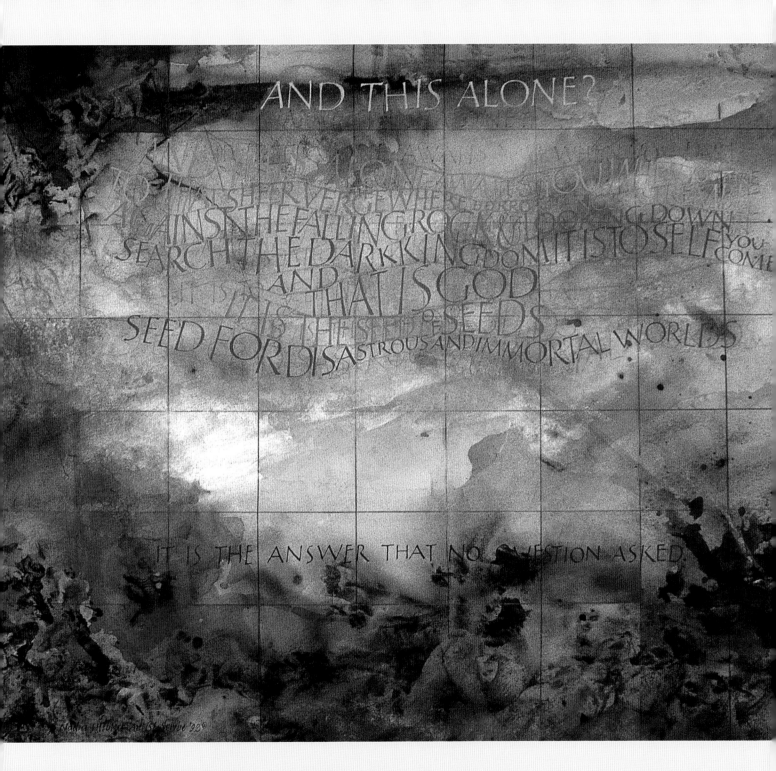

Roger Druet
Happiness within the moment

Acrylic on canvas.

Yves Leterme
But Be Doers of the Word

Brush and black ink freeform
italics.

Roger Druet
**Life is a little shadow crawling
through the grass and ending at
the sunset**

Acrylic on canvas.

Leonid Pronenko
The Brilliant World by Alexander Grin

Cyrillic script. Broad pens, flat brush, gouache on black paper.

Leonid Pronenko
Devoted to Edgar Allen Poe's Poetry

Broad pens, gouache, on black paper.

We can do
no great things
Only small things
with great Love.

Mother Teresa

Izumi Shiratani
Only Small Things

Chinese ink and brush freeform
italics on paper, gold leaf.

Leonid Pronenko
Composition

Freeform Roman capitals in gouache, with flat brushes on black paper.

Leonid Pronenko
Calligraphic Abstraction devoted to Edgar Allen Poe's poem *Eldorado*

Freeform Roman capitals in gouache, with flat brushes on black paper.

GILDING

THE TRADITIONAL SKILLS OF LAYING GOLD LEAF FOR A FLAT OR RAISED EFFECT REMAIN A FASCINATION TO CALLIGRAPHERS. EXPERIMENTS WITH NEWER GLUES, AND WITH EFFECTIVE GOLD SUBSTITUTES, HAVE BROADENED OUR SCOPE AND ENCOURAGED US TO FIND NEW WAYS TO INCORPORATE A SPARKLE, IN ADDITION TO GILDED INITIAL LETTERS.

Janet Mehigan
J, June

Watercolour, raised gold leaf on PVA versal, watercolour paper.

Jan Pickett
Woodland Dragon

Gold leaf on gesso versal, shell gold and gouache dragon, on stretched vellum.

Jan Pickett
Chinese Firedragon

Gold leaf on gesso versal, shell gold and gouache dragon, on stretched vellum.

Tim Noad
Illuminated letter "N"

Sponged gouache on vellum, letter in raised gold leaf on gesso. Flourish in powdered gold.

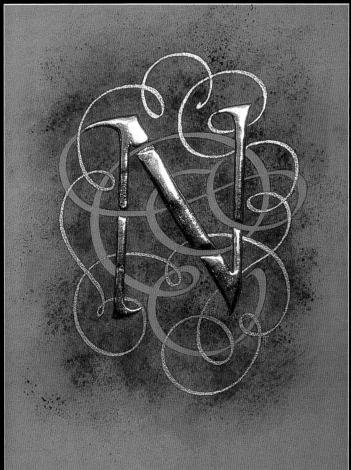

Veiko Kespersaks
DIOS

Brush lettering, raised PVA
gilding, on handmade paper.

Mary Noble
GOD

Gold leaf on acrylic gold size,
gold gouache lines, edged and
pointed brushes, gouache on
dyed tissue.

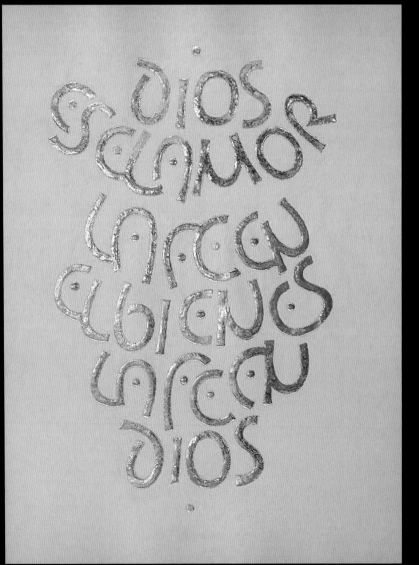

THE PRIDE OF THE PEACOCK IS THE GLORY OF GOD

Gemma Black
Who is your God

Maureen Sullivan
Peacock

Neil Bromley
Royal Barge

The Royal Barge of King John, reproduced on vellum.

Neil Bromley
St Peter

Interpretation of a Stained glass image. Gold leaf on vellum.

Ann Bowen
Illuminated Hebrew carpet page

Hebrew lettering, raised gold leaf, shell gold and gouache on vellum.

Jacqueline Lee
Wedding invitation with gold cross

Higgins Eternal ink, flourished copperplate script.

Mrs Oliver Samuel Heard, junior
requests the honour of your presence
at the Nuptial Mass uniting her daughter
Eleanor Anne
and
Mr Daniel Monroe Gilbane
in the Sacrament of Holy Matrimony
Saturday, the fifth of October
Two thousand and two
at three o'clock in the afternoon
Mission San José
San Antonio, Texas
Seated Dinner and Dancing to follow
San Antonio Country Club

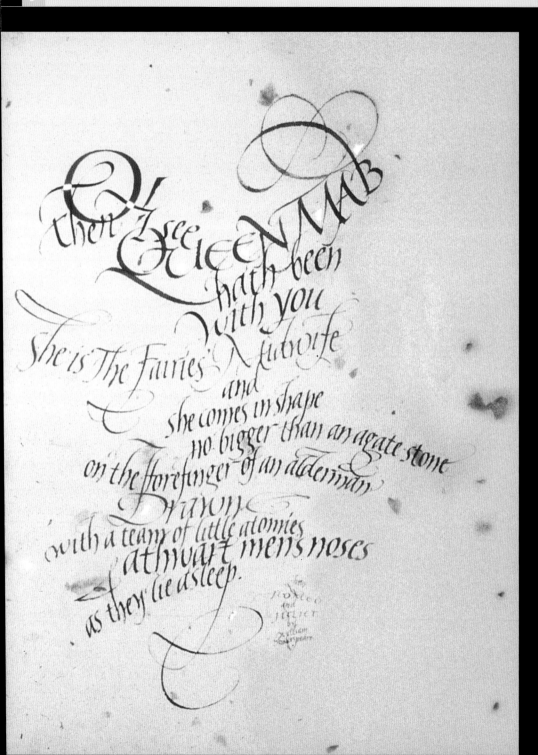

Jenny Hunter Groat
Queen MAB

Watercolour, gouache, quill, gold leaf
flourished italics on rose-petal HM paper.

Neil Bromley
King Arthur roundel

The Arms of the Twelve Knights of the Round
Table. Gold leaf on vellum.

Jan Pickett
Heraldic Achievement, Vale of Glamorgan

Gold leaf on gum ammoniac, shell gold,
gouache, on Arches Aquarelle paper.

HIC · JACET · ARTHURUS · QUONDAM REXQUE · FUTURUS

...The Armorial Bearings of King Arthur, king of all England, and the Knights of the Round table ...

Paula Comparini
Library painting, Cardinal George Basil Hume OSB

Drawn and painted versals. Raised gold on gesso, shell gold, watercolour and gouache, on stretched vellum.

Neil Bromley
Illuminated letter "S"

Gold leaf and gouache on vellum.

Janet Mehigan
D, December
S, September

From The Pageant of the Seasons and the Months manuscript book. Raised gold leaf on PVA, watercolour and gouache, on paper.

Mike Kecseg
Mystic Art

Gothic, italicized copperplate, and drawn versals. Pointed pen, broad-edge pen, stick ink, gouache, gold.

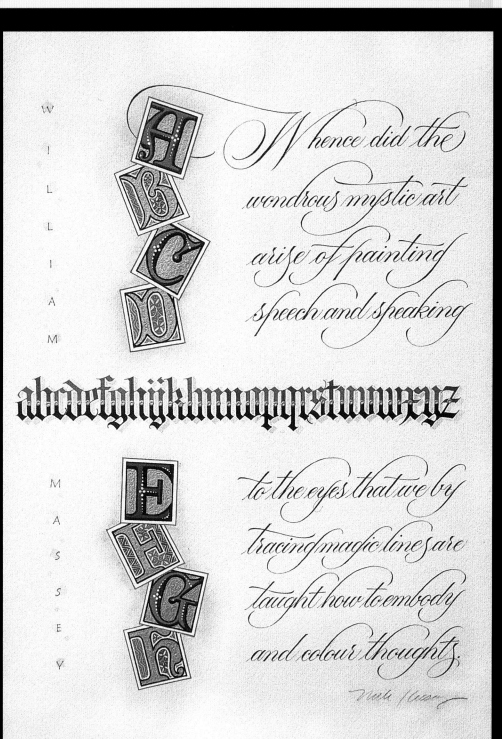

Viva LLoyd
Angel

Copy from thirteenth-century Psalter, St. Michael with serpent in letter "E". Shell gold, gouache on vellum.

Viva LLoyd
Noah's Ark

Copy from thirteenth-century Psalter, Strasbourg, letter "D". Raised and burnished gold on gesso, gouache, on vellum.

Cherrell Avery
Letter "L"

Traditional methods and style of Flemish fifteenth-century illuminated initials. Colour pigments with glair and gold leaf on gesso.

Janet Harper
George Thomson

Based on early fifteenth-century manuscript. Raised gold on gesso, gouache and stick ink, on vellum.

Death, be not proud,
though some have called thee
mighty and dreadful;
for thou art not so.

D O N N E

Sleep after toil, port after storming seas, peace after war, Death after life does greatly please

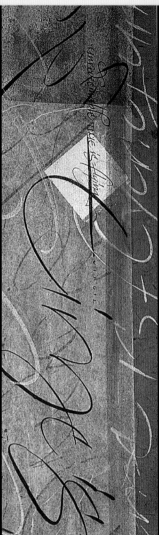

Mary Noble
Time is Flying

Pointed brush, Sumi ink and gold
paint freeform italic on rice
paper, collaged over gold leaf.

Izumi Shiratani
Death, be not proud

PVA, acrylic and balsa wood pen
background, gold gouache.
Gothic and italic text.

By inward
goads you
stirred me to
make me find
it unendurable
until through
my inward
perception, you
were a cer-
tainty to me.

I turned my
gaze on other
things I saw
that to you
they owe their
existence &
that in you
all things
are finite:

There is no purpose, there can
be no purpose to my life.
That's the earnest conclusion.
In between, there I go, never
really knowing where I am going
on why. I am little comfort to
myself although I am the only
comfort I have, excepting perhaps streets, clouds, the sun,
the faces and voices of kids
and the aged, and similar
accidents of beauty, innocence,

truth and loneliness. I consider nobody alive greater than
myself, and I know that I
am nothing sometimes arro-
gantly, sometimes decently,
with a tender feeling for any
form of life near death. I am
sick of myself and have good
reason to be. I was born into
this sickness, and I began to
notice it surely before I was
three. There wasn't enough to
ŏ me.

But when in
my arrogance
I rose against
you & ran up
against the
Lord, even
those inferior
things came on
top of me and
pressed me
down, and
there was never
any breathing
space on
relaxation.

As I gazed
at them, they
attacked me
on all sides
in massive
heaps.

Rose Folsom
**The Witness, unique
manuscript book**

Gouache and gold leaf
flourished italics on Arches
black cover paper, turkey quill,
PVA base for the gold.
Collection of the San Francisco
Public Library.

Marlene Gray
Handmade book

Tissue paper dyed with tea,
walnut ink lightweight capitals;
circles gold leaf on acrylic gold
size applied with a brush.

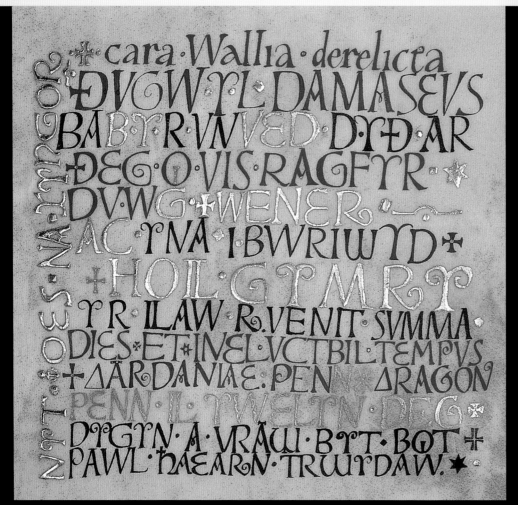

Valerie Dugan
GOLD

Built-up versals. Watercolour, transfer gold on gum ammoniac, on vellum.

Ann Bowen
Cara Wallia derelicta

Letters based on versal forms, in Welsh and Latin. Gold leaf on gesso, gouache, on vellum.

Gemma Black
An Irish blessing

Flourished italic lettering. Stick ink, Mitchell nibs, German gilding size, powdered gold, gouache on printmakers' paper.

Cherrell Avery
The Armenian Faith

Armenian alphabet and drawn and painted capitals. Layered gold leaf and waterproof ink on stretched vellum panel.

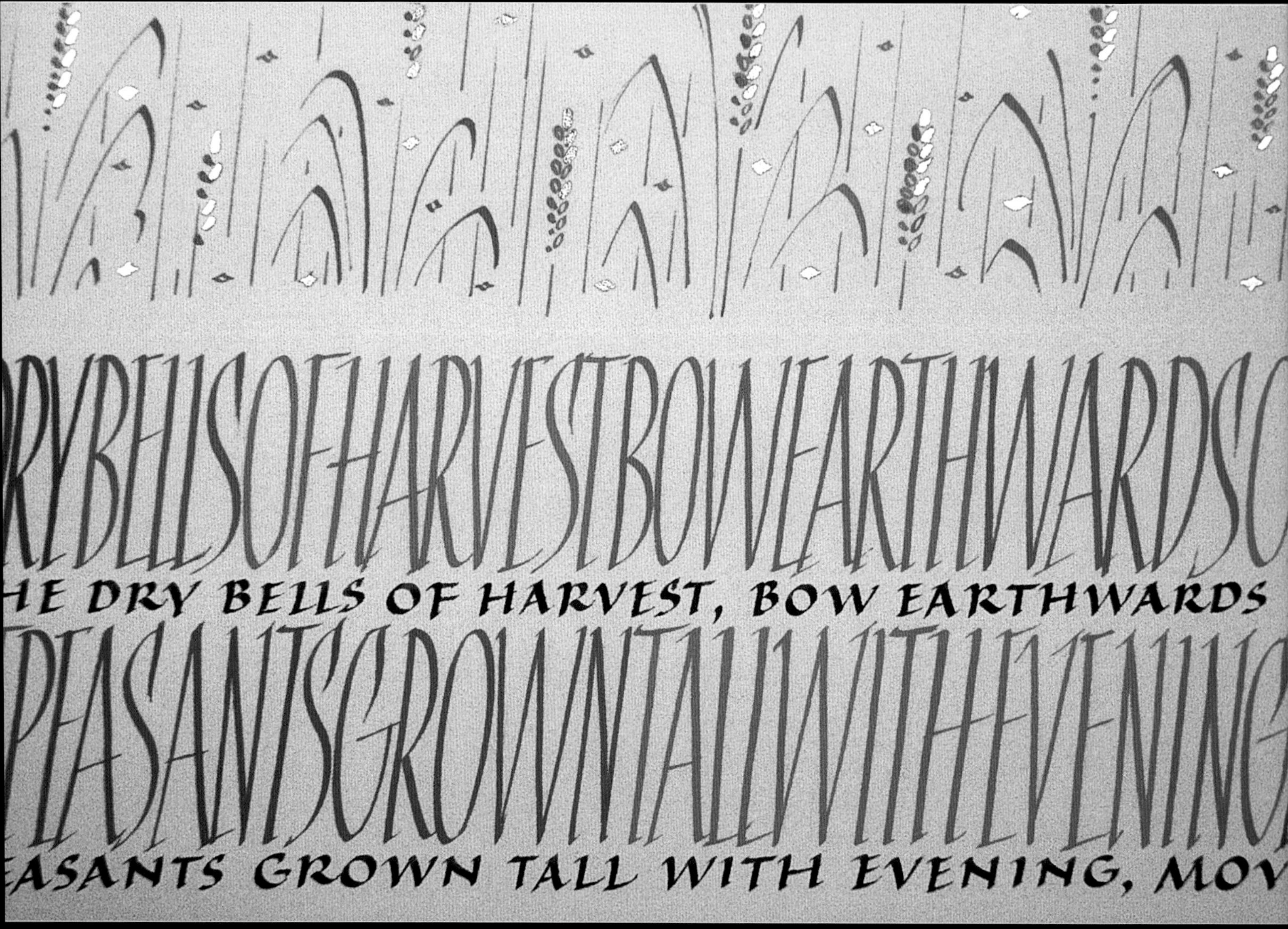

Janet Mehigan
The Cornfield by Phoebe
Hesketh (detail)

Veiko Kespersaks
You Have

Flat gilding, quill and gouache versals.

Tim Noad
Illuminated letter "S"

Sponged gouache on Arches paper, raised gold on PVA, flourishes in powdered gold.

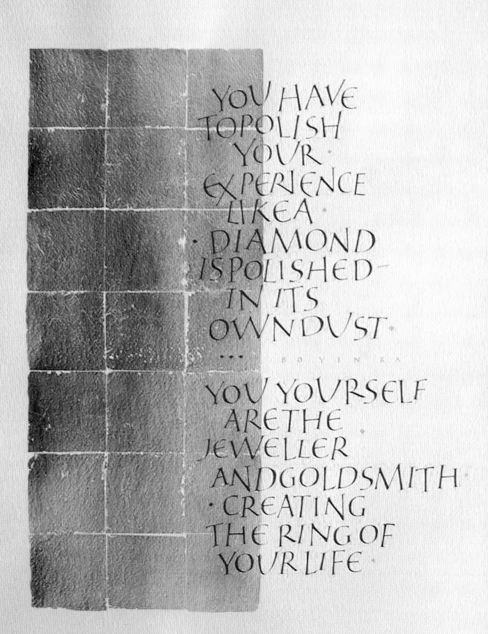

Nadia Hlibka
The Gilded Tin

Collage of gold leaf over acrylic on metal. Italic and various letterforms in gouache over and under gel transfer; acrylic, charcoal, colour pencil.

Neil Bromley
Medieval illuminated page of Saints' Days (September)

Illuminated versal initials and Gothic-based text. Gold leaf on vellum.

Nadia Hlibka
Prophecy is Brilliant Memory

Built-up pen-made versals. Raised gesso gilding; collaged image; gouache italic over acrylic and gouache.

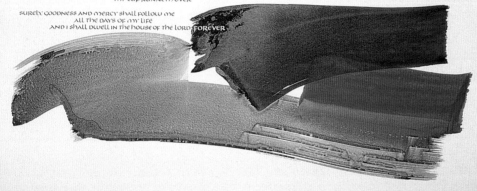

The Lord is my shepherd I shall not want

he maketh me to lie down in green pastures
he leadeth me beside the still waters

he restoreth my soul

he leadeth me in the paths of righteousness for his name's sake
Yea, though I walk through the valley of the shadow of death I will fear no evil for thou art with me
thy rod and thy staff they comfort me
thou preparest a table before me in the presence of mine enemies
thou anointest my head with oil

my cup runneth over

surely goodness and mercy shall follow me
all the days of my life
and I shall dwell in the house of the Lord FOREVER

Jenny Hunter Groat
23rd Psalm of David

Uncial lettering. Metal pen, brush, gold leaf on gum ammoniac, on crescent board.

Susan Richardson
We Are Stardust

Italic and Roman capital lettering. Gold and other acrylic paints on canvas.

Jan Pickett
Celtic Creation

Black gouache uncials, variegated Schlag (imitation metal leaf) on water gold size, Saunders Waterford paper.

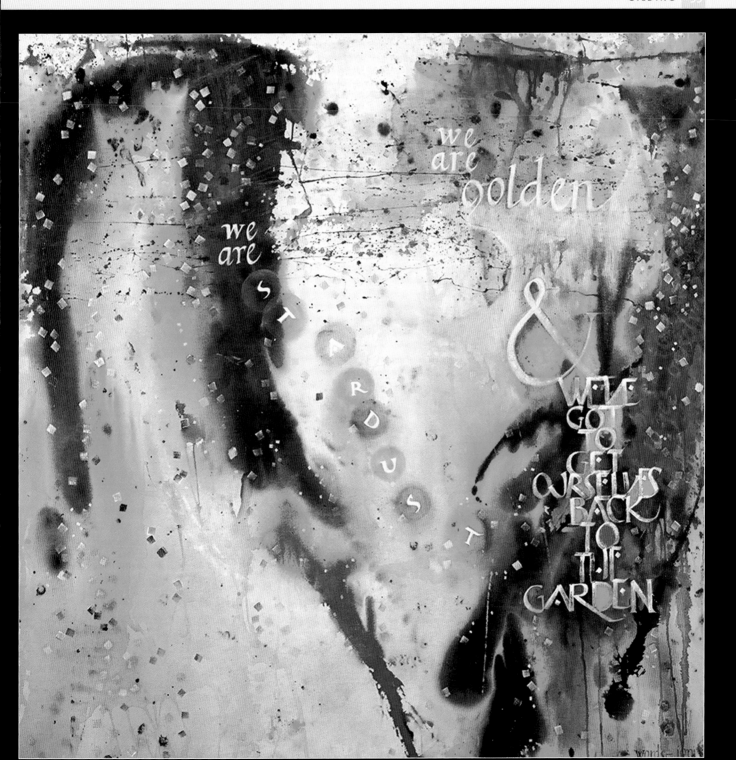

Lin Kerr
Nkosi Sikelela

Celtic ornamental capitals and versal lettering. 24c gold leaf on gesso, vellum laced onto wooden frame, gouache, pencil and acrylic impasto.

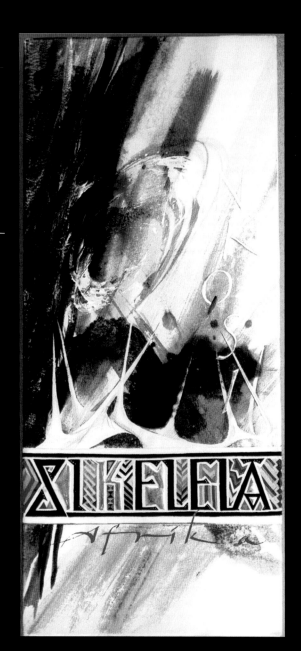

Lin Kerr
The Land

Freeform italic lettering. 24c gold leaf on gesso, vellum laced onto

Kathleen Armstrong
Celtic "Our Father"

Transfer gold on gum ammoniac uncials; image embossed then tinted.

Liesbet Boudens
La vie en rose

Built-up letters in gouache on Waterford paper.

Gemma Black
"R" love letter

Built-up versal. Watercolour paper with ink wash, Mitchell nib, fine rapidograph pen, German gilding size with powdered gold, tooled with metal stylus.

RESOURCES

SUPPLIERS

Winsor and Newton (Fine Art Materials)
ColArt Fine Art and Graphics limited
Whitefriars Avenue
Harrow HA3 5RH
UK
Tel: +44 (0)20 8424 3200
Web: www.winsornewton.com

John Neal Bookseller (Books, Calligraphy Tools
& Materials, Gilding Materials)
C1833 Spring Garden Street
Greensboro NC 27403
US
Tel: +1 800 369 9598
Web: www.JohnNealBooks.com

L. Cornelissen & Son (suppliers of gilding
materials, paints, inks and pens)
105 Great Russell Street
London WC1B 3RY
UK
Email: info@cornelissen.com
Web: www.cornelissen.com

W. Habberley Meadows (Gold Leaf)
5 Saxon Way
Chelmsley Wood
Birmingham B37 5AY
UK
Email: gold@habberleymeadows.co.uk
Web: www.habberleymeadows.co.uk

Blots Pen & Ink Supplies
14 Lyndhurst Avenue
Prestwich
Manchester M25 0GF
UK
Web: www.blotspens.co.uk

Falkiners Fine Papers (Papers, Artists and
Gilding Materials)
76 Southampton Row
London WC13 4AR
UK
Tel: +44 (0)20 7831 1151

Calligraphity (Calligraphy/Lettering Books)
Tel: +44 (0)1475 639668
Email: info@calligraphity.com
Web: www.calligraphity.com

CALLIGRAPHY SOCIETIES

Society of Scribes
P.O. Box 933
New York NY 10150
US
Tel: +1 212 452-0139
Email: info@societyofscribes.org
Web: www.societyofscribes.org

The Washington Calligraphers Guild
P.O. Box 3688
Merrifield VA 22116-3688
US
Web: www.calligraphersguild.org

Society for Calligraphy, Southern California
PO Box 64174
Los Angeles CA 90064
US
Web at www.societyforcalligraphy.org

Association for the Calligraphic Arts
1223 Woodward Avenue
South Bend, IN 46616
US
Fax: +1 574 233 6229
www.calligraphicarts.org

Society of Scribes and Illuminators (SSI)
6 Queens Square
London WC1N 3AT
UK
Email: scribe@calligraphyonline.org
Web: www.calligraphyonline.org

Calligraphy and Lettering Arts Society (CLAS)
54 Boileau Road
London SW13 9BL
UK
Tel: +44 (0)20 87417886
Web: www.clas.co.uk

Calligraphy Society of Victoria Inc
PO Box 2623
WGPO Melbourne
Victoria 3001 Australia
Email:callivic@alphalink.com.au
Web: www.alphalink.com.au/-callivic.

The Australian Society of Calligraphers Inc
PO Box 190 Willoughby
NSW 2068
Web:
www.australiansocietyofcalligraphers.com.au

Calligraphy Society of New Zealand
PO Box 3799
Christchurch
New Zealand

New Zealand Calligraphers
PO Box 99-674
Newmarket
Auckland
New Zealand

SUGGESTED OTHER READING

*Medieval Illuminators and their Methods of
Work* – Jonathan J. G. Alexander 1992
The Lindisfarne Gospels – Janet Backhouse 1981
Historical Scripts – Stan Knight 1984/1998
Lettering Art – Library of Applied Design –
Joanne Fink and Judy Kastin 1993
*Understanding Illuminated Manuscripts – A
guide to Technical Terms* – Michelle Brown 1994
The Art of Colour Calligraphy – Mary Noble and
Adrian Waddington 1994
A History of Illuminated Manuscripts –
Christopher de Hamel 1986/rep 1994
The Illuminated Page – Janet Backhouse 1997
*The Painted Page: Italian Renaissance Book
Illumination* – Jonathan J. G. Alexander 1994
The Art of Illuminated Letters – Tim Noad and
Patricia Seligman 1994
The Calligrapher's Companion – Mary Noble
and Janet Mehigan 1997
The Beginner's Guide to Calligraphy – Janet
Mehigan and Mary Noble 2001
The Book of Kells – Bernard Meehan 1997
Calligraphy, Illumination & Heraldry – Michelle
Brown & Patricia Lovett 2000
Calligraphy Techniques – Mary Noble 2001
Illumination for Calligraphers – Janet Mehigan
2001
Illuminated Scripts and their Makers – Rowan
Watson 2003
The Calligrapher's Bible – David Harris 2003
Calligraphy – Claude Mediaville 1996
Illuminating the Renaissance Thomas Kren and
Scot McKendrick 2003

GLOSSARY

Acrylic medium This modern adhesive dries clear. It is great for sticking metal leaf.

Arch The curved part of a letter as it springs from the stem.

Ascender The rising stroke of the letter which extends above the x-height as on b, d, h etc.

Baseline The bottom writing line on which the writing sits.

Body height This is also called the x-height and is the whole letter not including the ascender and descender.

Bowl of the letter The round or oval part of the letter formed by curved strokes as in R, a and p.

Broadsheet A design in calligraphy contained on a single sheet of paper or vellum.

Carolingian hand The first standard minuscule script, devised by Alcuin of York under the direction of Emperor Charlemagne at the end of the eighth century.

Cold-pressed paper (also Not) Paper made with a medium-textured surface.

Crystal parchment (also glassine) A transparent paper with a non-stick or resistant surface used when protecting gilding or gold surfaces.

Cursive This is a description of joined or linked writing formed by rapid and informal hand movements to create fluidity within the writing.

Descender Refers to the tail of the letter which extends below the line as in y or p.

Diaper patterns Designs created to ornament a surface with small patterns. The designs can cover plain painted backgrounds, adorn and enhance painted objects and materials, and emboss raised and flat gold surfaces.

Egg tempera Egg yolk added to powdered pigment colour to make paint.

Embossing To emboss means to indent a mark or pattern on gold or to create a raised or indented surface on paper with a tool through a stencil to make a design.

Endpapers These are the first and last folds of paper in a book, which are used to attach it to the cover.

Flourish An extended pen stroke or linear decoration used to embellish the basic letterform.

Gesso This is a compound made from plaster of Paris, glue and other ingredients which forms a raised surface on which layers of gold can be attached and polished.

Gouache This is watercolour paint (pigment and water) with an additional ingredient to make it opaque when used to give flat dense colour.

Gothic script A broad term embracing the angular styles of writing used in the late medieval period, late thirteenth century to the Renaissance.

Gum sandarac Lumps of gum, which when ground to a fine powder can be dusted lightly on to paper or vellum to improve the writing surface.

Hand This is an alternative term for handwriting or script.

Hot-pressed paper A smooth-surfaced paper.

Indent To leave a space additional to the usual margin when beginning a line of writing, as in the opening of a paragraph.

Interlinear spacing The spacing that occurs between two or more lines which allows sufficient space to accommodate ascenders and descenders.

Italic This slanting elegant script with oval compressed letterforms and springing arches evolved in the early fifteenth century, during the Italian Renaissance.

Layout The basic plan of a design showing spacing and organization of text.

Lowercase (see minuscule) The typological term for small letters as distinct from capitals or upper case.

Majuscule A capital or upper case letter.

Manuscript A term used specifically for a book or document written by hand rather than printed.

Minuscule A small or lower case letter.

PVA (Polyvinyl acetate) A clear adhesive which dries clear and can be used for sticking paper to paper and gold to paper.

Roman capitals The formal alphabet of capitals devised by the Romans and the basis of the Western alphabet systems.

Rough paper Paper which has an extremely pronounced texture when it is made.

Serif The beginning and the end part of the letter form.

Stem of the letter The main stroke of the letter.

Uncial hand A book hand used by the Romans and early Christians from the fourth century and based on very round, squat shapes.

Vellum Calfskin which has been limed, scraped and prepared for either writing or painting and illumination.

Versals Elegant capital letters made with a pen using compound strokes.

X-height The typographic term for the body height of the letter.

INDEX

Note: Page numbers in italics are for captions

CREDITS

The authors acknowledge that Winsor and Newton gouache and watercolour paints were used throughout the book

Quarto would like to thank the artists for kindly supplying their calligraphy and illumination reproduced in this book. All artists are acknowledged in the captions beside their work, except for the following:

(Key: l left, r right)
2   Liesbet Boudens
4   Jenny Hunter Groat
6l   An Vanhentenrijk
6r   Rose Folsom

All other photographs and illustrations are the copyright of Quarto Publishing plc. While every effort has been made to credit contributors, Quarto would like to apologize should there have been any omissions or errors – and would be pleased to make the appropriate correction for future editions of the book.